WORLD OF ANIMALS

1

MAMMALS

SMALL CARNIVORES

Raccoons, Weasels, Otters, Skunks...

PAT MORRIS, AMY-JANE BEER

GROLIER

Various members of the weasel family: European badger (1); European polecat (2); pine marten (3); wolverine (4).

Published 2003 by Grolier,
Danbury, CT 06816
A division of Scholastic Library Publishing

This edition published exclusively for the school and library market

Planned and produced by
Andromeda Oxford Limited
11–13 The Vineyard,
Abingdon, Oxon OX14 3PX

www.andromeda.co.uk

Project Director: Graham Bateman
Editors: Angela Davies, Penny Mathias
Art Editor and Designer: Steve McCurdy
Cartographic Editor: Tim Williams
Editorial Assistants: Marian Dreier, Rita Demetriou
Picture Manager: Claire Turner
Picture Researcher: Vickie Walters
Production: Clive Sparling
Researchers: Dr. Erica Bower, Rachael Brooks, Rachael Murton, Eleanor Thomas

Origination: Unifoto International, South Africa

Printed in China

Library of Congress Cataloging-in-Publication Data

Morris, Pat.
    Mammals / [Pat Morris, Amy-Jane Beer, Erica Bower].
        p. cm. -- (World of animals)
    Contents: v. 1. Small carnivores -- v. 2. Large carnivores -- v. 3. Sea mammals -- v. 4. Primates -- v. 5. Large herbivores -- v. 6. Ruminant (horned) herbivores -- v. 7. Rodents 1 -- v. 8. Rodents 2 and lagomorphs -- v. 9. Insectivores and bats -- v. 10. Marsupials.
    ISBN 0-7172-5742-8 (set : alk. paper) -- ISBN 0-7172-5743-6 (v.1 : alk. paper) -- ISBN 0-7172-5744-4 (v.2 : alk. paper) -- ISBN 0-7172-5745-2 (v.3 : alk. paper) -- ISBN 0-7172-5746-0 (v.4 : alk. paper) -- ISBN 0-7172-5747-9 (v.5 : alk. paper) -- ISBN 0-7172-5748-7 (v.6 : alk. paper) -- ISBN 0-7172-5749-5 (v.7 : alk. paper) -- ISBN 0-7172-5750-9 (v.8 : alk. paper) -- ISBN 0-7172-5751-7 (v.9 : alk. paper) -- ISBN 0-7172-5752-5 (v.10 : alk. paper)
    1. Mammals--Juvenile literature. [1. Mammals.] I. Beer, Amy-Jane. II. Bower, Erica. III. Title. IV. World of animals (Danbury, Conn.)

QL706.2 .M675 2003
599--dc21

2002073860   Set ISBN 0-7172-5742-8

About This Volume

In this volume we introduce you to the basic features of all mammals. We then go on to cover several carnivore groups, from weasels to otters to skunks and mongooses, which are mostly distinguished by their small size. All carnivores tend to be alert, active, and rather fierce. They are natural-born killers, many of them smaller than the average domestic cat, yet no less dangerous to their prey.

Despite their small size, several species regularly kill animals larger than themselves. But being small also offers opportunities to exploit prey animals like insects, which are too small for the larger and more dramatic carnivores, such as lions and tigers (see Volume 2), to bother with. However, several species have a varied diet, ranging from fish to fruit. Small carnivores inhabit every continent (except Antarctica) and most major habitats, although only one—the sea otter—spends all its life in the sea. Many are adapted to tree climbing, where they pursue prey or lurk in ambush. Others live underground, emerging to hunt rodents and rabbits at night. Some small carnivores live in highly organized social groups, while others live alone. Some species are quite numerous, but others have been reduced to perilously low numbers as a result of hunting for their lustrous and valuable furs.

Contents

The red or lesser panda lives in temperate forests.

Various members of the raccoon family: a ringtail eating a lizard (1); coati (2); kinkajou (3).

How to Use This Set

World of Animals: Mammals is a 10-volume set that describes in detail mammals from all corners of the earth. Each volume brings together those animals that are most closely related and have similar lifestyles. So all the meat-eating groups (carnivores) are in Volumes 1 and 2, and all the seals, whales, and dolphins (sea mammals) are in Volume 3, and so on. To help you find volumes that interest you, look at pages 6 to 7 (Find the Animal). A brief introduction to each volume is also given on page 2 (About This Volume).

Article Styles

Articles are of three kinds. There are two types of introductory or review article: One introduces large animal groups like orders (such as whales and dolphins). Another introduces smaller groups like families (The Raccoon Family, for example). The articles review the full variety of animals to be found in different groups. The third type of article makes up most of each volume. It concentrates on describing individual animals typical of the group in great detail, such as the tiger. Each article starts with a fact-filled **data panel** to help you gather information at-a-glance. Used together, the three article styles enable you to become familiar with specific animals in the context of their evolutionary history and biological relationships.

Data panel presents basic statistics of each animal

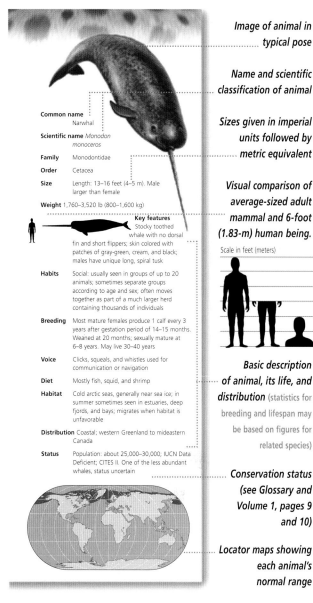

Image of animal in typical pose

Name and scientific classification of animal

Sizes given in imperial units followed by metric equivalent

Visual comparison of average-sized adult mammal and 6-foot (1.83-m) human being.

Basic description of animal, its life, and distribution (statistics for breeding and lifespan may be based on figures for related species)

Conservation status (see Glossary and Volume 1, pages 9 and 10)

Locator maps showing each animal's normal range

Article describes a particular animal

Scientific name of animal

Common name of animal

Captions to photographs provide additional information about each animal's lifestyle

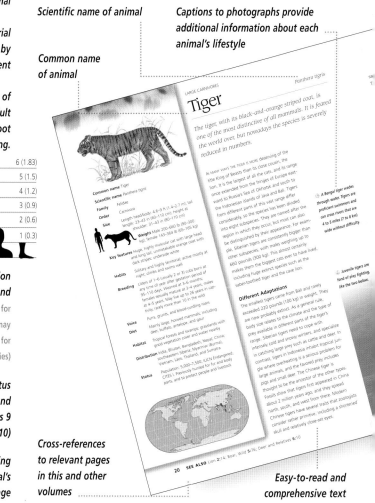

Cross-references to relevant pages in this and other volumes

Easy-to-read and comprehensive text

A number of other features help you navigate through the volumes and present you with helpful extra information. At the bottom of many pages are **cross-references** to other articles of interest. They may be to related animals, animals that live in similar places, animals with similar behavior, predators (or prey), and much more. Each volume also contains a **Set Index** to the complete *World of Animals: Mammals*. All animals mentioned in the text are indexed by common and scientific names, and many topics are also covered. A **Glossary** will also help you if there are words used in the text that you do not fully understand. Each volume ends with a list of useful **Further Reading and Websites** that help you take your research further. Finally, under the heading "List of Species" you will find expanded listings of the animals that are covered in each volume.

Introductory article describes family or closely related groups

SMALL CARNIVORES
The Raccoon Family

Meticulous drawings illustrate a typical selection of group members

Detailed maps clarify animal's distribution

At-a-glance boxes cover topics of special interest

Tables summarize classification of groups and give scientific names of animals mentioned in the text

Who's Who tables summarize classification of each major group and give scientific names of animals mentioned in the text

The Disappearing Tiger

Graphic full-color photographs bring text to life

Detailed diagrams illustrate text

Introductory article describes major groups of animals

WHALES AND DOLPHINS

Find the Animal

World of Animals: Mammals is the first part of a library that describes all groups of living animals. Each cluster of volumes in World of Animals will cover a familiar group of animals—mammals, birds, reptiles and amphibians, fish, and insects and other invertebrates. These groups also represent categories of animals recognized by scientists (see The Animal Kingdom below).

The Animal Kingdom

The living world is divided into five kingdoms, one of which (kingdom Animalia) is the main subject of the

World of Animals. Also included are those members of the kingdom Protista that were once regarded as animals, but now form part of a group that includes all single-cell organisms. Kingdom Animalia is divided into numerous major groups called Phyla, but only one of them (Chordata) contains those animals that have a backbone. Chordates, or vertebrates as they are popularly known, include all the animals familiar to us and those most studied by scientists—mammals, birds, reptiles, amphibians, and fish. In all, there are about 38,000 species of vertebrates, while the Phyla that contain animals without backbones (so-called invertebrates, such as insects, spiders, and so on) include at least 1 million species, probably many more. To find which set of volumes in the World of Animals is relevant to you, see the chart Main Groups of Animals (page 7).

Mammals in Particular

World of Animals: Mammals focuses on the most familiar of animals, those most easily recognized as having fur (although this may be absent in many sea mammals like whales and dolphins), and that provide milk for their young. Mammals are divided into major groups (carnivores, primates, rodents, and marsupials to name just

The chart shows the major groups of mammals in this set arranged in evolutionary relationship (see page 10). The volume in which each group appears is indicated. You can find individual entries by looking at the contents page for each volume or by consulting the set index.

Rodents (Order Rodentia): **squirrels, rats, mice Volume 7; cavies, porcupines, chinchillas Volume 8**

Lagomorphs (Order Lagomorpha): **rabbits, hares, pikas Volume 8**

Tree shrews (Order Scandentia): **Volume 9**

Insectivores (Order Insectivora): **shrews, moles, hedgehogs Volume 9**

Colugos, flying lemurs (Order Dermoptera): **Volume 8**

Primates (Order Primates): **lemurs, monkeys, apes Volume 4**

Pangolins (Order Pholidota): **Volume 9**

Carnivores (Order Carnivora): **raccoons, weasels, otters, skunks Volume 1; cats, dogs, bears, hyenas Volume 2**

Seals and sea lions (Order Pinnipedia): **Volume 3**

Odd-toed ungulates (Order Perissodactyla): **horses, rhinoceroses, tapirs Volume 5**

Even-toed ungulates (Order Artiodactyla): **pigs, camels Volume 5; deer, cattle, sheep, goats Volume 6**

Whales and dolphins (Order Cetacea): **Volume 3**

Bats (Order Chiroptera): **Volume 9**

Xenarthrans (Order Xenarthra): **anteaters, sloths, armadillos Volume 9**

Elephant shrews (Order Macroscelidea): **Volume 9**

Aardvark (Order Tubulidentata): **Volume 9**

Hyraxes (Order Hyracoidea): **Volume 8**

Dugongs, manatees (Order Sirenia): **Volume 3**

Elephants (Order Proboscidea): **Volume 5**

Marsupials: **opposums, kangaroos, koala Volume 10**

Monotremes (Order Monotremata): **platypus, echidnas Volume 10**

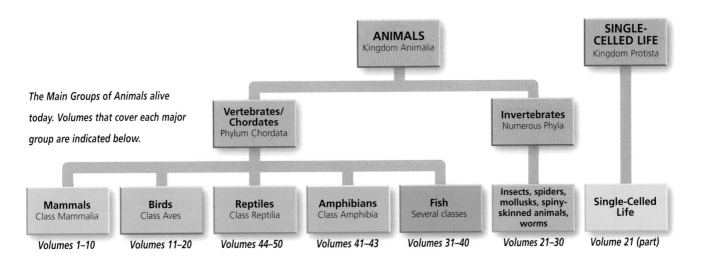

The Main Groups of Animals alive today. Volumes that cover each major group are indicated below.

ANIMALS Kingdom Animalia		**SINGLE-CELLED LIFE** Kingdom Protista

Vertebrates/ Chordates Phylum Chordata	**Invertebrates** Numerous Phyla

Mammals Class Mammalia	**Birds** Class Aves	**Reptiles** Class Reptilia	**Amphibians** Class Amphibia	**Fish** Several classes	**Insects, spiders, mollusks, spiny-skinned animals, worms**	**Single-Celled Life**
Volumes 1–10	Volumes 11–20	Volumes 44–50	Volumes 41–43	Volumes 31–40	Volumes 21–30	Volume 21 (part)

a few). All the major groups are shown on the chart on page 6. To help you find particular animals, a few familiar ones, such as sheep, goats, cats, and dogs, have been included in the chart.

Naming Mammals

To be able to discuss animals, names are needed for the different kinds. Most people regard tigers as one kind of animal and lions as another. All tigers look more or less alike. They breed together and produce young like themselves. This popular distinction between kinds of animals corresponds closely to the zoologists' distinction between species. All tigers belong to one species and all lions to another. The lion species has different names in different languages (for example, *Löwe* in German, *Simba* in Swahili), and often a single species may have several common names. For example, the North American mountain lion is also known as the cougar, puma, panther, and catamount.

Zoologists find it convenient to have internationally recognized names for species and use a standardized system of two-word Latinized names. The lion is called *Panthera leo* and the tiger *Panthera tigris*. The first word, *Panthera*, is the name of the genus (a group of closely similar species), which includes the lion and the tiger. The second word, *leo* or *tigris*, indicates the particular species within the genus. Scientific names are recognized all over the world. The scientific name is used whatever the language, even where the alphabet is different, as in Chinese or Russian. The convention allows for precision and helps avoid most confusion. However, it is also common for one species to apparently have more than one scientific name. That can be because a particular

species may have been described and named at different times without the zoologists realizing it was one species.

It is often necessary to make statements about larger groups of animals: for example, all the catlike animals or all the mammals. A formal system of classification makes this possible. Domestic cats are similar to lions and tigers, but not as similar as those species are to each other (for example, they do not roar). They are put in a different genus (*Felis*), but *Felis*, *Panthera*, and other catlike animals are grouped together as the family Felidae. The flesh-eating mammals (cats, dogs, hyenas, weasels, and so on), together with a few plant-eaters that are obviously related to them (such as pandas), are grouped in the order Carnivora. These and all the other animals that suckle their young are grouped in the class Mammalia. Finally, the mammals are included, with all other animals that have backbones (fish, amphibians, reptiles, and birds) and some other animals that seem to be related to them, in the Phylum Chordata.

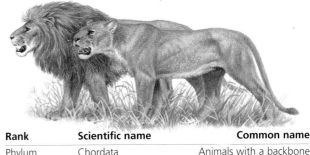

Rank	Scientific name	Common name
Phylum	Chordata	Animals with a backbone
Class	Mammalia	All mammals
Order	Carnivora	Flesh-eaters/carnivores
Family	Felidae	All cats
Genus	*Panthera*	Big cats
Species	*leo*	Lion

The kingdom Animalia is subdivided into phylum, classes, orders, families, genera, and species. Above is the classification of the lion.

WHAT IS A MAMMAL?

Mammals are warm, furry creatures that evolved from reptiles millions of years ago. They include humans, seals, shrews, mice, grass-eating cows and carnivorous tigers, flying bats and swimming otters. In fact, they have diversified to become the most successful of all animal groups. The secret of that success lies in the combination of special characteristics in mammals that sets them apart from the rest of the animal kingdom.

Mammals are a comparatively new group of animals; many others have a much more ancient origin. Reptiles, for example, first appeared millions of years earlier, and fish date back more than 400 million years.

The Origin of Mammals

About 200 million years ago a group of small reptiles began to develop the special features that would later enable mammals to dominate the animal world. Fossil remains provide clear evidence of some of the changes. The limbs became more upright, supporting the body from below rather than sprawling out to the side as in lizards and crocodiles. The skull developed more powerful jaws, and "spare" bones that were no longer needed as part of the lower jaw instead became bones in the ear, greatly enhancing hearing ability. The simple teeth of reptiles gradually became more diverse, enabling mammals to exploit a much wider range of foods than reptiles can cope with. Brain capacity enlarged too, probably associated with increased intelligence and more complex and sociable behavior. Less apparent from fossils are other important changes that must have taken place progressively. They include the production of active offspring instead of eggs and the secretion of milk to nourish the newborn young. Hair and fur also developed, enabling mammals to colonize cold places and become nocturnal. Such feats are difficult for reptiles, since they depend on sunshine to keep warm. The first mammals were small and insignificant creatures. Looking like today's solenodons and gymnures, they fed on insects caught at night.

Body Temperature

Mammals are often described as "warm-blooded." Reptiles and even some fish are also warm inside, but they cannot maintain a high blood temperature without basking in the sun or constantly moving around to generate heat from their muscles. Mammals, on the other hand, are "homeothermic," meaning that their inner temperature is not only high but kept constant. It is usually held at about 95 to 100°F (35 to 38°C) throughout the animal's life. The warmth is generated internally, so mammals are independent of heat from the sun. Homeothermy also provides protection from low temperatures, making it possible for mammals to live at high altitudes and in polar regions. Mammals can also be

⬆ *Adaptability, opportunism, and intelligence, plus the capacity for intricate social relationships, are traits that typify mammalian success. All are found in the red fox.*

⬅ *Fossils from the early Eocene (49 million years ago) were found at Lake Messel, Germany. The reconstruction on the left shows a community at the dawn of the age of mammals: Archaeonycteris, the first known bat (1); Messelobunodon, an ancestral artiodactyl (2); Propalaeotherium, an ancestral horse (3); Lepticidium, an insectivore (4); Paroodectes, a miacid (5); Eurotamandua, an anteater (6); Pholidocercus, a hedgehog (7).*

active at night, and that probably enabled them to escape competition with the dominant reptiles of the day.

Body heat is easily lost, especially from small animals that have a relatively large surface area in comparison to their mass. So there are benefits to being big; several evolutionary lines produced very large mammals, culminating in the blue whale, the largest animal that has ever lived. Elephants and various extinct giants also benefit from size, not least because few predators can touch them once they are full-grown. Large mammals are also efficient in energy terms, needing less food per pound of body weight than small ones. But they require a greater total quantity of food and will soon eat everything within reach unless they move on. A big body can be a handicap because moving around becomes progressively more difficult with larger size. Big animals also put greater stress on their bones and bodies, especially when moving

⬆ *Mammals must expend energy to warm or cool themselves. Elephants lose body heat by flapping their ears so that cool air flows over the blood vessels, and by splashing in water.*

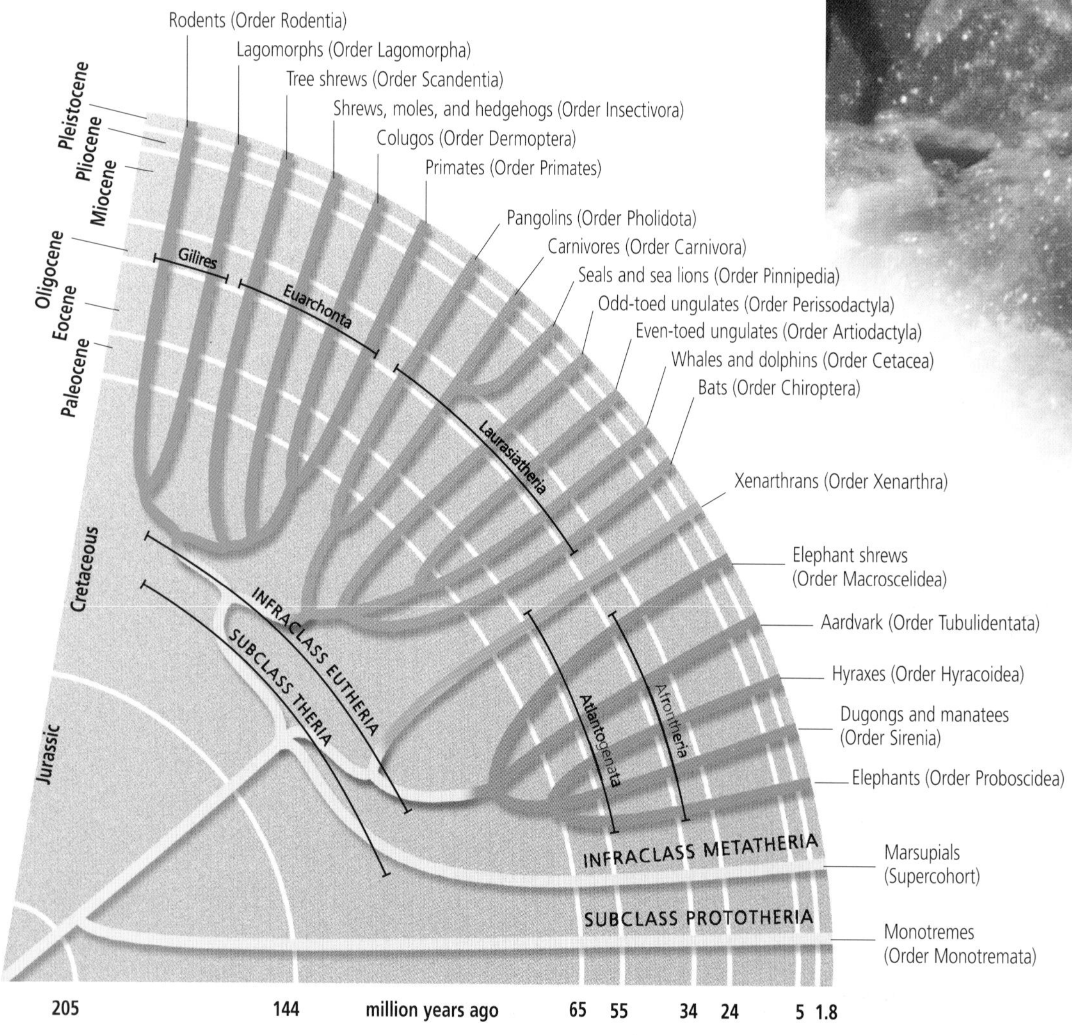

⬅ *The chart shows the evolution of mammals between the Jurassic era (205 million years ago) and the Pleistocene era (nearly 6 million years ago).*

Chart labels:

Rodents (Order Rodentia)
Lagomorphs (Order Lagomorpha)
Tree shrews (Order Scandentia)
Shrews, moles, and hedgehogs (Order Insectivora)
Colugos (Order Dermoptera)
Primates (Order Primates)
Pangolins (Order Pholidota)
Carnivores (Order Carnivora)
Seals and sea lions (Order Pinnipedia)
Odd-toed ungulates (Order Perissodactyla)
Even-toed ungulates (Order Artiodactyla)
Whales and dolphins (Order Cetacea)
Bats (Order Chiroptera)
Xenarthrans (Order Xenarthra)
Elephant shrews (Order Macroscelidea)
Aardvark (Order Tubulidentata)
Hyraxes (Order Hyracoidea)
Dugongs and manatees (Order Sirenia)
Elephants (Order Proboscidea)
Marsupials (Supercohort)
Monotremes (Order Monotremata)

Pleistocene
Pliocene
Miocene
Oligocene
Eocene
Paleocene
Cretaceous
Jurassic

Glires
Euarchonta
Laurasiatheria
Atlantogenata
Afrotheria
INFRACLASS EUTHERIA
SUBCLASS THERIA
INFRACLASS METATHERIA
SUBCLASS PROTOTHERIA

205   144   million years ago   65 55   34 24   5 1.8

10

The Diversity of Mammals

There are at least 4,500 species of mammals (but about 8,000 species of birds and over 20,000 fish). More than half of all known mammal species are rat-sized or smaller. One-third are rodents (rats, mice, squirrels, and so on), while one in five is a bat. The smallest mammal (Kitti's hog-nosed bat) weighs only a twentieth of an ounce (1.5 g). The Etruscan shrew is scarcely larger, and both are smaller than many beetles. The largest mammal (the blue whale) weighs a hundred million times as much. The naked mole rat stays in a single burrow for the whole of its life, but whales and fur seals may travel over 10,000 miles (16,000 km) on annual migrations. Some mammals live solitary lives except when they meet to mate; others form colonies numbering thousands. Yet others live permanently in tightly organized social systems in which each individual knows its place. Some mammals have only one young at a time, often at intervals of over a year, but many mice breed almost continuously. Mammals run faster than anything else on land. They also dig, fly, and swim. They range from the poles to the equator and from deserts to the open oceans. They eat grass, flesh, fruit, blood, fish, bamboo, insects, nectar, and gum. They shout, sing, and stay silent. Many have highly complex social behavior. Some defend territory with sophisticated scent-marking and recognition systems, while others live communally. Mammals are truly the world's most diverse and adaptable group of creatures.

Kitti's hog-nosed bat is the world's smallest mammal.

➲ **This chart lists the world's major groups of mammals.**

CLASS: MAMMALIA—2 subclasses, 27 orders, 139 families

SUBCLASS: Theria (Livebearers)
INFRACLASS: Eutheria (Placentals)
Order: Carnivora—carnivores: 240 species in 92 genera and 8 families
Order: Pinnipedia—seals and sea lions: 33 species in 21 genera and 3 families
Order: Cetacea—whales and dolphins: 85 species in 41 genera and 14 families
Order: Sirenia—dugongs and manatees: 4 species in 2 genera and 2 families
Order: Primates—strepsirhines, tarsiers, monkeys, and apes: 260 species in 64 genera and 13 families
Order: Scandentia—tree shrews: 18 species in 6 genera and 1 family
Order: Dermoptera—colugos: 2 species in 1 genus and 1 family
Order: Proboscidea—elephants: 3 species in 2 genera and 1 family
Order: Hyracoidea—hyraxes: 7 species in 3 genera and 1 family
Order: Tubulidentata—aardvark: 1 species in 1 genus and 1 family
Order: Perissodactyla—odd-toed ungulates: 16 species in 6 genera and 3 families
Order: Artiodactyla—even-toed ungulates: 196 species in 82 genera and 10 families
Order: Rodentia—rodents: over 1,990 species in 431 genera and 28 families
Order: Lagomorpha—lagomorphs: 81 species in 12 genera and 2 families

Order: Macroscelidea—elephant shrews: 15 species in 4 genera and 1 family
Order: Insectivora—insectivores: 423 species in 67 genera and 6 families
Order: Chiroptera—bats: over 900 species in 174 genera and 18 families
Order: Xenarthra—xenarthrans: 29 or 30 species in 13 genera and 4 families
Order: Pholidota—pangolins: 7 species in 1 genus and 1 family

INFRACLASS: Metatheria (Marsupials)
Order: Didelphimorphia—American opossums: 63 species in 15 genera and 1 family
Order: Paucituberculata—shrew opossums: 5 species in 3 genera and 1 family
Order: Microbiotheria—monito del monte: 1 species in 1 genus and 1 family
Order: Dasyuromorphia—Australasian carnivorous marsupials: 64 species in 18 genera and 3 families
Order: Notoryctemorphia—marsupial moles: 2 species in 1 genus and 1 family
Order: Peramelemorphia—bandicoots: 21 species in 8 genera and 2 families
Order: Diprotodontia—possums, wallabies, kangaroos, wombats, and koala: 125 species in 38 genera and 10 familes

SUBCLASS: Prototheria (Egg-layers)
Order: Monotremata—monotremes: 3 species in 3 genera and 2 families

rapidly or if they stumble on uneven ground. Consequently, there has to be a compromise, and land mammals cannot be much larger than an elephant without exceeding the limits of what their bodies can support. In the water things are different. Buoyancy removes most of the effects of gravity, enabling the great whales to be much larger than land creatures. But they in turn become limited by the problems of managing a gigantic body, pumping blood through enormous lengths of veins and arteries, distributing oxygen to tons of muscles, and conducting nerve impulses along nerves that may be over 60 feet (18 m) long.

Body heat can be conserved by using insulation. In mammals it is done by having dense layers of fine fur, sometimes with layers of fat under the skin for extra protection. Fur is a feature of mammals and cannot be found in any other group of animals. Long hairs protect from rain and snow, while woolly underfur keeps the animal warm. Dense fur allows the muskox to survive arctic blizzards and to stand out in the open all its life. Fur also enables mammals to keep warm and yet be quite small. Tiny mammals can exploit the possibilities of living in nooks and crannies away from predators and sheltered from the elements. Small size also permits greater activity, allowing squirrels and monkeys to leap among the treetops. In addition, it ensures the efficient use of tiny things for food, such as ants and small seeds.

Body warmth has many advantages over cold-bloodedness. Nerves work faster, enabling much greater activity, increasingly complex behavior, and more rapid reactions. Warmth also allows muscles to contract more quickly, making it possible to run fast and even to fly. Digestion is also more rapid, and digestive enzymes can work with greater efficiency if temperatures are kept high and constant. So, body warmth is not just about feeling comfortable; it is in fact essential to many of the major aspects of mammalian success. In conjunction with their warm body, mammals also have a highly efficient blood circulatory system. Their blood circulation works faster and at higher pressures than in all other animals except birds, constantly delivering enough food and oxygen to the tissues to allow them to function fully.

Reproduction

Mammal offspring are born as active babies and so avoid the perilous process of laying eggs and incubating them in the same place for weeks on end. Newborn young are fed on milk secreted by the mother's mammary glands, structures that are not present in any other group of animals. Milk allows rapid growth, especially in seals and whales. Shrews manage to raise a litter of babies that weigh more than the mother that feeds them. Milk is nourishing and fatty, but milk produced within the first hours after birth also has other benefits in the form of immune proteins. They provide valuable protection for the young animals against infection by germs.

⊙ *This idyllic scene of Hanuman langurs grooming and young playing hides a sinister side of their society. When new males take over a group, they may kill the infants of their predecessors.*

Feeding the babies on milk requires the mother to look after them. Parental care, sometimes involving the male too (although he never produces milk), is normal among mammals and another big benefit. It allows the young to learn from their parents, enabling them to know what is dangerous, where to go, and what to eat without them having to find out the hard way (perhaps with fatal results). Parental care sometimes lasts for many years, especially in primates, and contributes to the fact that a

Infanticide

The killing of young by members of their own species (infanticide) is one of the most arresting examples of aggression in the animal kingdom. It has been recorded in over 100 mammal species. The possible benefits are varied and depend on species. In chimps, which eat their victims, such behavior may simply be to obtain food. In lions a male that kills a rival's offspring brings the bereaved mother into breeding condition so he can mate with her.

→ *Skeleton of the gray wolf, which fits a general mammal pattern. This basic bony equipment is modified to serve the particular requirements of more specialized species, such as the horse, whale, and bat.*

high proportion of a mammal's total behavioral repertoire may be learned rather than inherited. In contrast, reptiles and birds inherit most of their behavioral patterns with their genes and learn relatively little. The advantage is that learned behavior is flexible and can be adjusted to meet all sorts of conditions and circumstances. Inherited behavior, on the other hand, tends to be stereotyped and inflexible and not necessarily appropriate to a different way of life.

Mammal families are generally small, normally fewer than 10 young, and sometimes only one. As a result, the young are well looked after and tend to achieve a high survival rate. Many species also live in social groups in which individuals cooperate to raise babies more successfully than they might on their own.

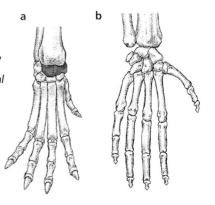

→ *Wrists in which the scaphoid, lunar, and central bones are fused to form the scapholunar bone are typical of carnivores (a). In primates, such as humans (b), the bones remain independent, allowing greater flexibility.*

Diversity and Exceptions

Some of the features described above are found among certain nonmammalian groups, but no other animals have them all. Curiously, some mammals have given up one or more of their special advantages. For example, whales and naked mole rats are nearly hairless as an adaptation to their particular way of life. In the case of whales insulation is provided by large amounts of fat (blubber) under the skin. Mole rats protect themselves from the cold by living in very warm burrows. Echidnas and the platypus are exceptional, too, in that they produce eggs instead of giving birth to babies, but they still nourish their young with milk. When food is seasonally scarce, hedgehogs, bats, and other hibernators abandon homeothermy. At such times the animals do not have enough energy to maintain a high body temperature, and so hibernating is an advantageous behavior.

The basic mammal body plan—including four feet, each with five toes—has been modified to allow the development of highly efficient diggers, runners, swimmers, and fliers. The teeth are also specialized to

cope efficiently with many different kinds of food, from meat to nuts, leaves, fish, grass, blood, and insects. Again, there are exceptions associated with special lifestyles. Ant-eating species, such as the aardvark or giant anteater, have reduced teeth or none at all, since their tiny food needs no chewing. Instead, a long, sticky tongue is required to gather the insects.

The special characteristics of mammals enable them to live in a wide variety of habitats more independently of their surroundings (air temperature, for example) than any other animals. Mammals are found everywhere, from the polar regions to deserts, mountaintops, and jungles. Some make prolonged dives into the deep sea, while others may fly many miles each night or walk hundreds of miles on annual migrations. Mammals can survive successfully in a wider diversity of habitats than any other animal group. One mammal (*Homo sapiens*) has even landed on the moon, something that no other animal has ever achieved! Some mammals have become abundant and widespread. A few are so successful and numerous that we treat them as pests because they compete with humans for food or destroy what we have produced for ourselves. Horses, dogs, cattle, and sheep have also played a major role in helping humans in our own social evolution and successful conquest of the planet. Domesticated mammals, in exchange for regular food, shelter, or healthcare, provide us with useful services, such as transportation and muscle power, or products, like meat, milk, and leather. Such items would cost us a lot more effort to obtain by other means. Some mammals (like rats) are significant carriers of diseases that endanger many people, but some primates and laboratory mice assist medical research to combat disease among humans.

Challenging Present, Uncertain Future

Today we live in the age of mammals. This group now dominates the world, effectively replacing the reptiles and amphibians that were once the major land animals. Those that remain are reduced to relatively few species living a comparatively restricted range of lifestyles. However, over the last 1 to 2 million years enormous changes have taken place in the variety of mammal species in different parts of the world. Many have become extinct, and many others have been reduced to critically small numbers. The decline is mainly due to the overwhelming success of just one mammal species—our own. Today we humans manipulate the environment on a global scale and, with it, all species that share the world with us.

Mammals have suffered heavily from persecution by people, particularly species considered to be dangerous like the tiger or wolf. Large mammals are at risk because they need a lot of space and eat a great deal of food every day. The same land cannot support elephants, for example, and also produce crops for people. Expansion of farmland has reduced the numbers of wild animals everywhere and forced them back into less suitable habitats. Fences, built to keep mammals out of crops, force them to live in areas that cannot support such high numbers. Wild mammals that steal from crops planted on the land they

⊕ *A lion killing a buffalo. Even when agape, the jaw can deliver suffocating or bone-splitting pressure. The meat-shearing teeth are then used to cut the flesh.*

⊕ *Carnivores, as in this wolf, typically have 44 teeth, consisting of three incisors (1), one canine (2), four premolars (3), and three molars (4). The last upper premolar and first lower molar have sharp tips and high cusps to shear through flesh. Jaw power (right) is crucial for the capture and tearing up of prey. The massive temporalis muscle (a) delivers the power to suffocate or crunch through bone. The masseter muscle (b) provides the force needed to cut and grind flesh when the jaws are almost closed.*

carnivore (wolf)

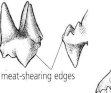

meat-shearing edges

used to occupy are shot or snared. As numbers of humans have increased, wild mammals have been pushed aside. At the same time, numbers of domestic mammals, especially cattle, sheep, and goats, have greatly increased in numbers, replacing their wild relatives. Some wild mammals have been specially hunted for their skins, ivory, or other valuable products. Catastrophic population declines have resulted, particularly among the larger species because they take a long time to reach breeding age or often produce few young. They cannot compensate easily for the large numbers killed, and many have now reached the verge of extinction. About one-quarter of all known mammals are significantly threatened in some way. That is roughly twice the proportion of threatened birds.

Categories of Threat to Animals

Two types of classification are used throughout this set regarding conservation status: IUCN categories and CITES Appendices. They appear, where relevant, in the data panel for each species.

The IUCN

With so much conservation activity in different countries it is important to have a worldwide overview, some way of coordinating what goes on in different parts of the planet. That is the role of the International Union for the Conservation of Nature (IUCN), also referred to as the World Conservation Union. The mission of the IUCN is to influence, encourage, and assist societies throughout the world to conserve the diversity of nature and natural systems. It seeks to ensure that the use of natural resources is fair and ecologically sustainable. Based in Switzerland, the IUCN has over 1,000 staff and the help of 10,000 volunteer experts from 181 countries.

Perhaps the best-known role of the IUCN is the production of the Red Lists of Threatened Species. First published in 1966, the books were designed to be easily updated, with details of each species appearing on a different page that could be removed and replaced as new information came to light. So far, the Red Lists include information on over 18,000 types of animal, of which over 11,000 are threatened with extinction. Gathering such a vast amount of information is a huge task, but it provides an invaluable conservation resource. The Red Lists are now available in CD-ROM format and on the World Wide Web. Governments throughout the world use them when assessing conservation priorities and in policymaking.

In the data panel for each species in this set there is a section on status. Some animals, for example, many rodents and bats, are abundant and not at risk. In such cases an IUCN listing is not relevant. Where an animal is known to be officially at risk, its IUCN rating is given. All categories of threat have been taken from information provided in the latest Red Lists.

It should be pointed out that while IUCN categories draw attention to the status of rare species, they do not confer any legal protection. That is done through national laws, and internationally by CITES.

IUCN CATEGORIES

EX **Extinct**, when there is no reasonable doubt that the last individual of a species has died.

EW **Extinct in the Wild**, when a species is known only to survive in captivity or as a naturalized population well outside the past range.

CR **Critically Endangered**, when a species is facing an extremely high risk of extinction in the wild in the immediate future.

EN **Endangered**, when a species faces a very high risk of extinction in the wild in the near future.

VU **Vulnerable**, when a species faces a high risk of extinction in the wild in the medium-term future.

LR **Lower Risk**, when a species has been evaluated and does not satisfy the criteria for CR, EN, or VU.

DD **Data Deficient**, when there is not enough information about a species to assess the risk of extinction.

NE **Not Evaluated**, species that have not been assessed by the IUCN criteria.

Note: The Lower Risk (LR) category is further divided into three subcategories. Conservation Dependent (cd): species that are the focus of continuing species-specific or habitat-specific conservation programs the cessation of which would result in the species qualifying for one of the threatened categories within a period of five years; Near Threatened (nt): species that do not qualify for Conservation Dependent, but which are close to qualifying for VU; and Least Concern (lc): species that do not qualify for the two previous categories.

CITES

CITES is the Convention on International Trade in Endangered Species of Wild Fauna and Flora (also known as the Washington Convention, since it was signed after a meeting in Washington, D.C., in 1975). Currently 152 nations have agreed to implement the CITES regulations. Trading in animals and their body parts has been a major factor in the decline of some of the world's rarest species, and CITES aims to control the problem.

CITES lists (called Appendices) tally species that are threatened by international trade. Animals are assigned to Appendix I when all trade is forbidden. Any specimens found alive or dead (including skins, feathers, and so on) will be confiscated by customs at international borders, seaports, or airports. Appendix II species can be traded internationally, but only under strict controls. Wildlife trade is often valuable in the rural economy, and that raises difficult questions about the relative importance of animals and people. Nevertheless, traders who ignore CITES rules risk heavy fines or imprisonment. Some rare species—even those with the highest IUCN categories (many bats, for example)—may have no CITES protection simply because they have no commercial value. Trade is then not really a threat. Further details of the categories are shown in the table CITES Appendices.

CITES APPENDICES

Appendix I lists the most threatened traded species, namely, those that are heading toward extinction and will be harmed by continued trade. Such species are usually protected in their native countries and can only be imported or exported with a special permit. Permits are required to cover the whole transaction—both exporter and importer must prove that there is a compelling scientific justification for moving the animal from one country to another. This includes transferring animals between zoos for breeding purposes. Permits are only issued when it can be proved that the animal was legally acquired and that the remaining population will not be harmed by the loss.

Appendix II includes species that are not currently threatened with extinction, but that could easily become so if trade is not carefully controlled. Some common animals are listed here if they closely resemble threatened species, since criminals could try to sell the rare species pretending they were a similar common one. Permits are required to export such animals, with requirements similar to those for Appendix I species.

Appendix III species are those that are at risk or protected in at least one country. Other nations may be allowed to trade in the animals or their products, but they will probably need to prove that they come from safe populations.

⊖ *In the 1960s and 1970s hundreds of thousands of ocelots were killed for their skins, and coats made from ocelot pelts sold for tens of thousands of dollars. Trade has now been curtailed as a result of CITES restrictions imposed in 1989.*

SMALL CARNIVORES

The order Carnivora includes some of the most exciting and formidable predators on earth. Some, such as those included in Volume 2, are very large. However, size is not everything, and the majority of the Carnivora are natural-born killers, despite being smaller than the average house cat.

Origins

The earliest Carnivora were small, tree-dwelling animals, not unlike today's civets (Viverridae). They evolved from insectivore ancestors some 50 million years ago. Although carnivores are naturally absent from Antarctica, Australia, and New Zealand, some species have been introduced there.

Characteristics

Not all members of the Carnivora are purely carnivorous (meat-eating animals), but there are a number of other characteristics that set them apart from other mammal groups. Fittingly for a group composed mainly of predators, the most reliable "diagnostic features" of carnivores are their teeth. Whatever the animal's size, there are four canine teeth, which tend to be long, pointed, and curved slightly backward to help stab prey while gripping it firmly. Carnivores also have a set of four shearing teeth (carnassials), including the last upper premolars and the first lower molars. Carnivore jaws are muscular, but unlike those of most herbivores (animals that feed on vegetable matter), the jaws can only move in a simple open-and-shut fashion. Large food items are usually ripped or gnawed into pieces and swallowed without much chewing. The plant material eaten by some species can be pounded between the grinding surfaces of the molars. However, the teeth and gut of carnivores are not well suited to a vegetable diet, since they have only a simple stomach and short intestine.

All carnivores have four or five digits on each foot, but in some species the first digit ("thumb" or "big toe") is reduced to a dewclaw. Of the smaller species, most walk on the sole of the foot, but some—such as the genets—walk on their toes.

Being Small

The four families of small carnivores covered in this volume include some quite large animals—the wolverine and the giant otter both frequently exceed 3 feet (90 cm) in length. However, as a general rule, animals in these groups are small, light, and nimble. The smallest of all, the least weasel, can measure as little as 5.5 inches (14 cm) from nose to tail tip and weigh just under an ounce (28 g). For a predatory animal such small size might seem like a disadvantage, but what weasels and their relatives lack in stature they more than make up for in speed, agility, and ferocity. They readily tackle prey several times their own bodyweight, which is unusual in any group of animals. They can also squeeze into tiny spaces, enabling them to reach prey in nests, burrows, and crevices that would foil larger hunters.

Lifestyle

Small carnivores can be solitary (like the stoat) or social (like meerkats and coatis). Smell is important in communication, and most species use scent to mark home ranges and territories and to convey personal information to other members of their species. The sense of smell is also important in hunting, as is vision. Most small carnivores climb well, and some spend almost their entire life in trees. Most can swim, and a few

are semiaquatic, most notably the otters, whose special adaptations to the water include webbed feet, dense, waterproof fur, and a powerful, rudderlike tail. The sea otter spends most of its life in the water and may not even come ashore to give birth.

Reproductive strategies vary widely, but in the majority of species rearing offspring is the job of the female. Compared with other small animals, the young spend a long time with their mother, gaining strength and learning the skills they will need in adult life. Play is an important part of growing up, and games often involve parents as well as offspring.

← *A group of banded mongooses find a vantage point on a termite mound in the Masai Mara Nature Reserve, southern Kenya.*

The Raccoon Family

Raccoons are medium-sized, long-bodied mammals with a long tail. Although there are only 19 different species in the family Procyonidae, its members display a remarkable diversity in their appearance and ecology. Only the kinkajou has a uniform body color. The rest have distinctive coats with various facial markings and ringed (banded) tails.

What Is a Raccoon?

The raccoons are descended from ancestors of the dog family, Canidae. Their origin is reflected in the family name Procyonidae, which comes from the Greek words *pro*, meaning "before," and *kuon*, meaning "dog." Recognizable fossils of raccoon ancestors have been found dating back 20 million years—to a time when Europe and North America were one continent. As the continents separated, the raccoon family was split unequally, with the procyonids remaining in the New World (the Americas) and the subfamily Ailurinae, ancestors of the red panda, in the Old World (the Eastern Hemisphere, excluding Australasia).

Raccoons have five toes on each foot, with the third toe being the longest. They are flat footed and walk partly or entirely on the soles of their feet, like bears. The red panda, however, has an extra digit, which functions as a thumb. Generally, the claws do not retract like those of most cats, except in ringtails and red pandas, which have semiretractile claws on their forepaws.

The procyonids range in size from the slender ringtail, weighing little more than 1.8 pounds (0.8 kg), to the stockier raccoon, which can reach 33 pounds (15 kg).

Despite being classified as carnivores, most of the raccoon family eat surprisingly little meat. Fruit makes up the bulk of their diet, although they often supplement it with a variety of insects and small animals. The kinkajou tops up its fruit diet with the occasional insect, while red pandas feed mainly on bamboo shoots, fruit, roots, lichen, and acorns. Raccoons will eat fish, crayfish, snails, and worms as well as berries, nuts, and fruit; and the olingo preys on small birds and mammals. The most carnivorous of the procyonids are the ringtail and cacomistle. They have well-developed, doglike carnassial teeth to catch and slice up prey as large as rabbits. The diet of procyonids is reflected by their external appearance. For example, the kinkajou has a shorter than average muzzle with a long tongue for obtaining nectar from flowers. In contrast, the coatis have long, flexible snouts to probe for insects.

Family Procyonidae: 3 subfamilies, 7 genera, 19 species

RACCOONS AND COATIS 4 genera, 12 species

Procyon 7 species, including common raccoon (*P. lotor*); crab-eating raccoon (*P. cancrivorus*)

Nasua 2 species, ringtailed coati (*N. nasua*); white-nosed coati (*N. narica*)

Nasuella 1 species, mountain coati (*N. olivacea*)

Bassariscus 2 species, ringtail (*B. astutus*); cacomistle (*B. sumichrasti*)

KINKAJOU AND OLINGOS 2 genera, 6 species

Potos (kinkajou) 1 species (*P. flavus*)

Bassaricyon (olingo) 5 species, including *B. gabbii* (no common name); *B. alleni* (no common name)

RED PANDA 1 genus, 1 species

Ailurus red panda (*A. fulgens*)

SEE ALSO Raccoon, Common **1**:22; Coati, Ringtailed **1**:28; Panda, Red **1**:30

⤓ *Various members of the raccoon family: a ringtail eating a lizard (1); a coati sniffing for insects (2); a kinkajou licking nectar from a flower while gripping a branch with its prehensile tail (3).*

3

⤒ *A pair of ringtails. The species was originally reared as a mouser in prospectors' camps in the early American West, hence its alternative name of "miner's cat."*

Where Raccoons Live

The procyonids (excluding the red panda) occupy a diversity of habitats ranging through most of North, Central, and South America. The ringtails and cacomistles are found mainly in rocky cliffs and dry forests, while coatis prefer more wooded regions. Olingos are found in American tropical rain forests, while the adaptable raccoons thrive in all of these habitats. The red panda is confined to Asia, favoring remote, high-altitude forests. All procyonids are nocturnal, except the coatis, which are mainly active during the day.

Lifestyle

Procyonids can live for 10 to 15 years in captivity, but generally no more than seven in the wild. While males wait until their second year to breed, females usually do so in their first spring. They give birth in dens or nests and provide all the parental care. At birth the young weigh only about 5 ounces (142 g) and are poorly developed. Most species have litters of three or four, but red pandas produce only one or two young at a time, and kinkajous usually only one.

Recent studies of the raccoon family in the wild reveal that their social structure is complex. Species such as the coati move around in large social groups. Others, like the ringtail, seem to be more solitary. While some of the Procyonidae—such as the common raccoon—are thriving, others are classified by the IUCN as Endangered. The red panda, olingo, and cacomistle are among those in decline as a result of destruction of forest habitats.

Common name
Common raccoon

Scientific name
Procyon lotor

Family Procyonidae

Order Carnivora

Size Length head/body: 18–27 in (45–68 cm); tail length: 8–12 in (20–30 cm); height at shoulder: about 10–12 in (25–30 cm). Male about 25% larger than female

Weight 11–18 lb (5–8 kg), but sometimes up to 33 lb (15 kg)

Key features Black "bandit" face mask, accentuated by gray bars above and below; black eyes; short, rounded ears; bushy tail with alternate brown and black rings (usually 5); body hairs long and gray

Habits Nocturnal; mainly solitary, although related females may live close to one another

Breeding Four to 6 young born around February to April after gestation period of 63 days. Weaned at 7 weeks; females usually sexually mature by their first spring, males by 2 years. May live over 17 years in captivity, up to 16 in the wild

Voice Chitters, purrs, hisses, barks, growls, snarls, and squeaks

Diet Fruit, berries, nuts, and seeds; also fish, crayfish, clams, snails, and earthworms; crops such as corn and stored grain

Habitat Almost anywhere in North America, including urban areas

Distribution Southern Canada, U.S., and Central America

Status Population: abundant. Most common member of raccoon family; continues to expand its range and increase in numbers

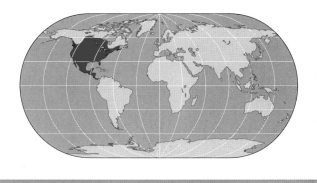

Common Raccoon

Procyon lotor

Raccoons are one of the most familiar North American animals. Their adaptability has allowed them to succeed in a wide range of habitats, while their appealing looks make them extremely popular with people.

THE RACCOON'S INTELLIGENCE, alertness, and curiosity were a source of fascination to early settlers and are celebrated in Native American folklore. Raccoons are often kept in captivity, and their speed of learning is thought to be somewhere between that of the rhesus monkey and the domestic cat. Young raccoons make intriguing pets, although as they mature, they can become quite a handful.

Masked Bandits

Raccoons are unmistakable animals, with their characteristic black "bandit" mask across the eyes and their bushy, banded tail. They have stout little bodies, typically weighing between 11 and 18 pounds (5 and 8 kg), although weights are known to change with season and distribution; northern animals are larger than southern ones. The heaviest raccoon recorded reached 62.4 pounds (28.3 kg).

Enormous numbers of raccoons have been trapped or shot for their skins, which are used to make jackets and hats. Raccoons are also kept in captivity to supply the fur trade. As a result of the financial gains to be made from fur farming, the common raccoon was introduced to France, the Netherlands, Germany, and parts of Russia in the 1930s and 1940s. Many escaped into the wild, and raccoons spread to Switzerland, Austria, and the Czech Republic. Some have also turned up in Poland, Hungary, Denmark, and Slovakia. The European raccoons are now sometimes considered a nuisance.

The raccoon's coat is made up of two types of hair. The short, fine underfur is uniformly

 SEE ALSO Coati, Ringtailed **1**:28; Panda, Red **1**:30; Old World Monkey Family, The **4**:40

gray or brownish and provides the animals with warmth and some protection from the wet. Growing from among its short coat are longer, stiffer guard hairs, which are tipped with black or white. The density of the guard hairs alters the overall appearance of the coat, often giving it a fuzzy or shaggy look. Raccoons molt in the early spring, with hair loss beginning at the head and proceeding along the back. New fur grows throughout the summer to provide extra warmth for the winter. Many raccoons have variable amounts of yellow in their coats, and some albinos have been reported. Apart from size the sexes are similar in appearance, and juveniles resemble adults. Raccoons are excellent climbers, aided by sharp claws and the ability to rotate the hind foot through 180 degrees (thereby turning it backward). Such ability makes them one of

ⓔ *The raccoon's "bandit" eye mask, brown-and-black ringed tail, and small, round ears are trademark characteristics of this highly distinctive species.*

Raccoon Currency

The raccoon's fur has always been the main reason for hunting and trapping the animal. During the 17th century bans were imposed to prevent too many raccoon skins being exported from the United States. At one time the skins were used as currency; and when the frontiersmen of Tennessee set up the state of Franklin, local officials received payments of "coonskins" each year. Although they are hard wearing, raccoon skins are not especially valuable nowadays, and trade in them is no longer a threat to population size. However, a movie about Davy Crockett, king of the wild frontier, created a sudden fashion for coonskin caps like the one worn in the movie, costing the lives of many raccoons!

only a few mammals that can hang by their hind feet and descend tree trunks head first.

Raccoons often use dens in hollow trees, preferring an entrance hole that is about 9 to 10 feet (3 m) above the ground. They also use ground burrows, brushy nests, old buildings, cellars, log piles, and haystacks in which to shelter and spend the day. In fact, they will nest almost anywhere that offers protection from predators and the weather. Each den is only used for a short period, except for over winter, when dens may be occupied for longer. When a mother has just given birth, she will also stay put, avoiding the risky and difficult business of moving her family.

Water Loving

Throughout their range raccoons are found almost everywhere that water is available. They are most abundant in forested and brushy swamps, mangroves, flood plain forests, and fresh and saltwater marshes. They are also common in cultivated and abandoned farmlands and can settle quite happily in suburban areas within parks and gardens. Raccoons are less common in dry upland woodlands, especially where pine trees grow. They also tend to avoid large open fields. Where they have spread out onto the prairies of the northern United States and southern Canada, they like to live in buildings and wet places. In desert areas they do not disperse far from rivers and springs. Raccoons are only rarely found at altitudes above 6,600 feet (2,000 m).

Raccoons do not hibernate, and in southern parts of their range they are active all year long. In the northern United States and southern Canada the coming of snow initiates periods of inactivity, although raccoons are easily roused in spells of warmer weather. During their winter sleep their heart rate does not decline, their body temperature stays above

Washing Bears

The raccoon's skillful forepaws are a prominent feature and are reflected in its name. The common name raccoon is derived from the Algonquian word *arakun*, which roughly translates as "he who scratches with his hands," a reference to the frequent grooming that raccoons characteristically indulge in. The German name *waschbär*, or "washing bear," refers to the raccoon's habit of washing its food. Even its scientific name *lotor* is taken from the Latin word *lavere*, meaning "to wash." The perception that raccoons wash themselves with their hands actually comes from observations of raccoons catching and feeding on aquatic prey. They dabble and splash in the water in an instinctive manner to catch fish, giving every appearance of washing their food. It is the same instinctive behavior displayed by captive raccoons (even when there is no water) that has encouraged the notion of the "washing bears."

The raccoon's forepaws have a well-developed sense of touch and are capable of delicate manipulation. In fact, the raccoon is almost as skillful as a monkey at handling its food.

95°F (35°C), and their metabolic rate remains high. As a result, they use more energy than true hibernators. Since they consume little or no food during their inactive period, their survival depends on the fat reserves they have built up over the previous summer and fall. In long and harsh winters raccoons may lose up to half of their body weight. Raccoons are often found denning together over winter, since they use less energy keeping warm when they snuggle up close. Up to 23 raccoons have been known to huddle together in a single den.

Raccoons are typically active from sunset to sunrise, although there is a peak in feeding activity just before midnight. Raccoons living by coastal marshes may be seen feeding during the day when their food source of crustaceans and mollusks is exposed at low tide. Raccoons are opportunists, able to make a meal from whatever food is available. It is their ability to take advantage of so many kinds of food that is the secret of their success.

In most areas plants provide the main food eaten by raccoons, especially fleshy fruit, berries, nuts, and seeds. They will also eat earthworms and insects and sometimes stored grain. Corn is a particular favorite and is usually taken just before it is ripe and ready for human consumption. Raccoons also eat small birds and sometimes snakes and lizards. Where they live near turtle nesting beaches, they will dig up and steal the buried eggs. They will also eat other vertebrates such as gophers, squirrels, shrews, rabbits, and mink; but such animals are usually already dead, so the raccoons just feed from the corpse. Raccoons occasionally scavenge the remains of larger mammals such as deer, cows, and even horses.

Breeding

Raccoons become sexually mature in their first spring, although some (particularly males) do not breed until their second season. Mating can be from December through August, occurring later in the season farther south. The peak of the breeding season is usually between February and March, with most litters being born a few weeks later in April and May. The later in the year a litter is born, the less chance the young have to fatten up for winter. Inability to survive the winter may be a factor that limits the spread of raccoons farther north.

At birth raccoons weigh about 2 to 3 ounces (60 to 75 g) and measure about 4 inches (10 cm) in length. They are covered in hair, although the mask and tail rings are represented only by dark-pigmented skin. After about three weeks they open their eyes, squirming actively and making chittering noises. Their legs become strong enough for walking by the fourth to sixth week. Their first molt occurs at seven weeks, when they shed the infant coat, and the adult fur begins to grow.

Weaning takes place from seven weeks, and the young start to leave the nest and forage for themselves. They may still be suckled by their mother for up to four months. By fall juveniles may weigh up to 15 pounds (7 kg),

⊕ Raccoons often forage beside rivers, lakes, or marshy areas where they feed on fish, crayfish, clams, snails, and other aquatic animals. They also take readily to water and are strong swimmers.

City Slickers

The raccoon's adaptability has enabled it to thrive in a variety of human-dominated environments. In fact, it has become very familiar to city dwellers. However, these masked bandits are notorious for raiding garbage bins. Not only are they known to carry away whole bins, but the nimble-fingered raiders have also learned to untie ropes used to secure the bins, rather than bite through them.

The secret of the common raccoon's success is that it can make a meal of almost any available food, including the contents of garbage baskets.

but full size is not reached until the second year. Families generally share a den over winter, and the young raccoons will leave their mother by the spring. Few wild raccoons live more than five years, but some survive up to 16 years. The oldest recorded captive raccoon was still living after 20 years.

⊕ *Two young raccoons by their nest in a hollow tree. As they gain independence and start to look for their own food, their mother will move them to a den at ground level to prevent them from falling.*

Social Organization

The social organization of raccoons is not well known, although adults are generally solitary. However, several females—usually closely related—will live in areas that overlap, but they still tend to avoid each other. One or more males will also inhabit the same area and mate with the resident females. During the breeding season females mate with between one and four males. There is competition between males for mating privileges, with heavier males gaining greater access to the females. One successful male is likely to be responsible for over half the

matings in his range, with the smaller males securing a few matings each.

Males may live alone or in small groups and will occupy a distinct territory ranging in size from 125 to 12,500 acres (50 to 5,000 ha). In general, raccoons will roam over 1,500 acres (600 ha) in a year. Males may travel together; but they disperse during the breeding season, when fighting and competition between them increase. Social relations are probably established and signaled through various postures, vocalizations, and scents. At least 13 different calls have been identified in raccoons. Sounds are used between individuals in close proximity to each other. Mothers keep in touch with their young by purring sounds, while hissing, short barks, and snorts express fear.

Despite the success of the common raccoon, several related species—such as the Cozumel Island raccoon (*Procyon pygmaeus*) from southeastern Mexico—are listed by the IUCN as Endangered. The Barbados raccoon (*Procyon gloverellani*) is said to have become extinct sometime after the 1960s. However, there is little to compromise the survival of the common raccoon. Predators such as wolves, bobcats, pumas, great horned owls, and alligators may pose a small threat, but few raccoons actually fall prey to them. Common raccoons are also hunted for sport (known as "coon hunting"), but relatively few are killed.

The main cause for concern is the common raccoon's susceptibility to certain diseases that can be transmitted to humans, such as leptospirosis, tularemia, and most commonly (and worst of all) rabies. The common raccoon is the major carrier of rabies in the southeastern United States and in 1997 accounted for half of all reported cases of rabies from wild animals in the whole country. Raccoons also often host a type of parasitic roundworm that is harmless to the raccoon itself, but may cause death in domestic animals and even in small children.

⊖ *The common raccoon is so familiar in North America that it is often the topic of TV cartoons. A successful species, it is expanding in both range and numbers.*

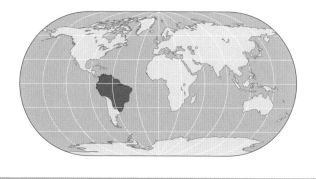

Common name Ringtailed coati (coatimundi)

Scientific name *Nasua nasua*

Family Procyonidae

Order Carnivora

Size Length head/body: 16–26 in (41–67 cm); tail length: 12.5–27 in (32–69 cm); height at shoulder: up to 12 in (30 cm). Male generally larger than female

Weight 7–13 lb (3–6 kg)

Key features Long, flexible snout; long, banded tail; stocky, reddish-brown to black upper body, yellowing underneath; coat has coarse, long hairs; distinctive white muzzle, chin, and throat

Habits Active throughout the day; females form gangs with juveniles; males are often solitary

Breeding Births occur mainly April to June, perhaps earlier farther south; 2–7 young born after gestation period of about 74 days. Weaned at 4 months; sexually mature at 2 years. May live over 17 years in captivity, 9–15 in the wild

Voice Grunts and chittering used to maintain contact with group, also snarls and squeaks; if threatened, will indicate alarm by barking

Diet Woodland invertebrates (such as earthworms, millipedes, and snails); frogs and lizards caught with forepaws; adult males tend to prey on large rodents; very fond of fruit

Habitat Woodlands

Distribution Colombia south to Argentina and Uruguay

Status Population: abundant. Generally common and widespread

Ringtailed Coati

Nasua nasua

The ringtailed coati is intelligent and sociable. Its Latin name, nasua, *means "nosy one" and aptly describes the inquisitive, long-snouted raccoon.*

AT FIRST GLANCE COATIS (often called coatimundis) resemble a slender version of their black-masked cousin, the common raccoon. Like raccoons, they have a distinctive banded tail and bold facial markings. Their forelegs are shorter than their hind legs, so coatis always seem to walk with their bottom held high in the air, accentuating their tapering tail, which is longer than their head and body. They have a long, flattish snout, which is particularly sensitive and flexible. It is well adapted to sniffing out insects and poking among stones and bits of rotten wood.

Coatis are found in woodland areas. They require vegetation for cover, since they are mainly active during the day, although adult males can also be active after dark. At night they sleep curled up in the trees. They are good climbers, using their tail to balance, and can rotate their ankles 180 degrees, enabling them to descend trees headfirst.

Fruit-Loving Carnivores

Ringtailed coatis generally travel about 1,600 to 2,200 yards (1,500 to 2,000 m) each day in search of their favorite food—fruit. When it is not available, they forage the forest floor, thrusting their snouts among the leaf litter in search of invertebrates, such as millipedes, earthworms, termites, snails, and tarantulas.

Coatis are the most sociable of the raccoon family. Females and juvenile males gather in bands of up to 20 individuals. However, males over two years old are normally solitary, except during the breeding season, and are usually excluded aggressively from bands by the adult females. In fact, they are so isolated that it was originally thought there were two kinds of animal—the coati, which lived in groups, and the coatimundi, which led a solitary life.

The bonds between females are strong, and all band members help take care of the young, not just their own or those closely related to them. The juveniles are well cared for, even after they leave the nest. Although coatis do not share food, the bands forage together so females can watch over and defend the young. Band members will groom each other, using their long claws as combs, picking parasites from each other's fur and gently nibbling with their teeth.

Bonding Sessions

In the breeding season adult males are accepted into bands, but behave submissively toward females. Males are also permitted into the band for a few days after the young are born, allowing them to become familiar with their young. What sounds like a friendly gesture is actually a defense mechanism. If males do not identify with their young, they may attempt to kill and eat them at other times of the year when they become more carnivorous.

Mating takes place once a year during a two- to four-week period. Pregnant females separate from the group to construct a tree nest, where they give birth to their young. Sometimes another female may climb up to the nest to assist in nursing the infants. The young open their eyes after 11 days and leave the nest at five weeks to join their mother and the rest of her group.

A similar species, the white-nosed coati, lives in Central America and extended its range north to Arizona. Numbers peaked in the 1950s and have since declined. Coatis are now scarce in the United States and declining in Mexico. Farther south, the ringtailed coati seems more secure, although it is threatened by habitat disruption. Coatis are generally tolerated because they rarely do any harm to livestock.

Coatis can be made into pets, although the practice is discouraged to prevent further reduction in wild populations. Captive coatis show high levels of intelligence, often causing trouble for zookeepers by unscrewing lamps and hoarding screws and bulbs as playthings.

⊕ *Ringtailed coatis are good climbers and sleep and nest in trees. They adopt two techniques for climbing, either ascending hand-over-hand or galloping up wide trunks with forefeet and hind feet clutching the bark. On the ground they move through the forest at a walk or gallop, holding their tail upright, except for the slightly drooping tip.*

Common name Red panda (lesser panda)

Scientific name *Ailurus fulgens*

Family	Procyonidae (sometimes considered a member of the bear family, Ursidae)
Order	Carnivora
Size	Length head/body: 20–24 in (50–60 cm); tail length: 12–20 in (30–51 cm); height at shoulder: about 10–12 in (25–30 cm)
Weight	6–13 lb (3–6 kg)
Key features	Vaguely raccoonlike animal the size of a large domestic cat; bright chestnut-colored fur, darker on belly; tail banded chestnut and cream; face has cream and white "mask"
Habits	Arboreal and nocturnal; spends most of day sleeping in trees and feeds there at night
Breeding	One to 4 young born in spring and summer (peaks in June) after gestation period of 114–145 days. Weaned at 4 months; sexually mature at 18 months. May live for 17 years in captivity, 8–14 in the wild
Voice	Normally silent
Diet	Bamboo shoots and leaves; fruit, berries, and flowers; birds, eggs, and small mammals
Habitat	Temperate forests, both deciduous and conifer, often on steep slopes
Distribution	Himalayan regions of Nepal, Bhutan, India, Laos, Myanmar (Burma), and China (Sichuan and Yunnan Provinces)
Status	Population: unknown, but unlikely to exceed a few thousand; IUCN Endangered; CITES I

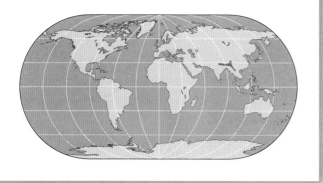

Red Panda *Ailurus fulgens*

The red panda is a puzzling creature, sharing many features of raccoons, bears, and its more famous cousin, the giant panda.

THERE HAS BEEN MUCH DEBATE among zoologists about whether both panda species belong in the bear family (Ursidae), the raccoon family, (Procyonidae), or whether they should be classified in a family of their own—the Ailuridae. The red panda's DNA (genetic molecular structure) is distinctly bearlike, but the animal's general shape, size, and appearance are those of a raccoon. However, red pandas are more arboreal than raccoons, spending most of their time up in the trees.

Red pandas live in the mixed forests that grow on the lower slopes of the Himalaya Mountains at altitudes of between 6,500 and 15,750 feet (2,000 and 4,800 m) above sea level. It gets very cold at night, and the pandas have long, dense fur to help keep them warm.

Thumblike Structure

Like the giant panda, the red panda has an additional "thumb." One of the small bones in the wrist (called the radial sesamoid) has become enlarged to provide a thumblike structure against which the five true digits can grip and hold food. The pandas are also able to hold onto the branches of trees with ease. Although they are quite large, bigger than an average domestic cat, red pandas are excellent climbers: Their grip is so strong that they can scamper down tree trunks headfirst without falling off. Yet when they walk on the ground, they tend to have a waddling gait caused by their front legs being angled inward. Nevertheless, they can travel quite fast by bounding along; but when frightened, they will seek safety by climbing trees.

similar size. Red pandas also have a generally slow metabolism, which helps conserve energy. Unlike the giant panda, their diet is not completely restricted to bamboo. They will also eat the leaves, flowers, fruit, roots, and bark of other plants, and have been known to consume fungi. Occasionally they will catch and eat various small animals, including insects, and will also take birds' eggs or nestlings. Nevertheless, although they belong to a mainly carnivorous group of mammals, red pandas do not normally hunt animal food. They behave as inefficient herbivores instead.

Red pandas mate early in the winter, and the young are born about four and a half months later. A female gives birth in a tree hole or rock crevice to a small family of up to four cubs. She looks after them more or less continuously for about a week. After that she spends increasingly long periods away from the nest to feed herself, but returns regularly to suckle and clean her babies. After three months the young cubs are ready to leave the den. They go out each night, staying close to their mother, learning their way around and how to find food. They usually disperse before the breeding season arrives again. If they do not, the mother will drive her youngsters away.

Warning Displays

Red pandas live solitary lives; and when they do meet, they engage in a variety of raccoonlike displays. Actions include arching their back in a threatening manner, shaking their head, and snapping their jaws shut. Sometimes they will rear up on their hind legs with their front paws held high in the air.

Red pandas face many difficulties in their forest home. They are sometimes hunted and frequently get caught in traps intended for musk deer. However, the main threat facing red pandas today is the large-scale loss of their habitat as trees are felled for timber and to clear space for crops and livestock.

⊕ Deforestation is a problem throughout the red panda's range. However, efforts are now being made to conserve mountain forests, which may benefit the species.

Pandas have evolved from carnivorous (meat-eating) ancestors. However, they are mainly vegetarian and eat relatively little animal food. Yet the panda's digestive system is still basically that of a carnivore, with a simple stomach and a short intestine. Most plant-eating mammals have very long intestines in order to provide the maximum digestive efficiency needed to cope with fibrous plant food. Therefore much of the nutritional benefit in what the panda eats is wasted. Because of their inefficient digestion pandas have to eat a lot more than a specialized herbivore of a

The Weasel Family

Family Mustelidae: 6 subfamilies, 26 genera, 66 species

WEASELS, MINK, AND POLECATS 8 genera, 24 species

Mustela 16 species, including long-tailed weasel (*M. frenata*); least weasel (*M. nivalis*); stoat (*M. erminea*); black-footed ferret (*M. nigripes*); American mink (*M. vison*); European polecat (*M. putorius*)

Gulo 1 species, wolverine (*G. gulo*)

Vormela 1 species, marbled polecat (*V. peregusna*)

Ictonyx 1 species, zorilla (*I. striatus*)

Poecilictis 1 species, North African banded weasel (*P. libyca*)

Poecilogale 1 species, African striped weasel (*P. albinucha*)

Galictis 2 species, grison (*G. vittata*); little grison (*G. cuja*)

Lyncodon 1 species, Patagonian weasel (*L. patagonicus*)

OTTERS 7 genera, 13 species

Lontra 4 species, including North American river otter (*L. canadensis*); marine otter (*L. felina*)

Lutra 3 species, including hairy-nosed otter (*L. sumatrana*); spot-necked otter (*L. maculicollis*); Eurasian otter (*L. lutra*)

Lutrogale 1 species, smooth-coated otter (*L. perspicillata*)

Amblonyx 1 species, short-clawed otter (*A. cinereus*)

Aonyx 2 species, Cape clawless otter (*A. capensis*); Congo clawless otter (*A. congicus*)

Pteronura 1 species, giant river otter (*P. brasiliensis*)

Enhydra 1 species, sea otter (*E. lutris*)

SKUNKS 3 genera, 10 species

Mephitis 2 species, striped skunk (*M. mephitis*); hooded skunk (*M. macroura*)

Spilogale 3 species, including western spotted skunk (*S. gracilis*)

Conepatus 5 species, including western hog-nosed skunk (*C. mesoleucus*); Andes skunk (*C. chinga*)

MARTENS 2 genera, 9 species

Martes 8 species, including pine marten (*M. martes*); yellow-throated marten (*M. flavigula*)

Eira 1 species, tayra (*E. barbara*)

BADGERS 6 genera, 10 species

Mydaus 2 species, teledu (*M. javanensis*); Palawan stink badger (*M. marchei*)

Arctonyx 1 species, hog badger (*A. collaris*)

Melogale 4 species, including Indian ferret badger (*M. personata*)

Meles 1 species, European badger (*M. meles*)

Mellivora 1 species, honey badger (*M. capensis*)

Taxidea 1 species, American badger (*T. taxus*)

Typically, mustelids are small, fierce animals with long, thin bodies and short legs. Some, such as the sea otter, are quite large; others, like the least weasel (also known as the European common weasel), are small enough to live in mouse burrows. Mustelids form the largest family of carnivores and occur naturally throughout the world, except Antarctica, Australia, and some smaller islands.

What Is a Mustelid?

Mustelids evolved from the same basic ancestors as many other groups of carnivores, but their exact evolutionary history is somewhat obscure. Some zoologists believe that the skunks are sufficiently different to be classified in their own separate family—the Mephitidae.

Most mustelids attack and kill their own prey on land, but the various species of otters obtain the majority of their food (mainly fish) from the water. Some mustelids, particularly martens and badgers, are more omnivorous, eating a wide variety of fruit, nuts, and other vegetable material, as well as animal food.

To deal with such a variety of different foods, mustelids have a very varied dentition (arrangement of teeth). The badgers and wolverine have the most teeth (38), including broad and almost flat-topped molars for grinding solid food and even bones. More typically, the weasels have only 34 teeth, but they are needle sharp to stab their prey and tear it to pieces. The honey badger has the fewest teeth, with just 32.

Mustelids are characteristically smelly creatures. Skunks are notorious for the stench they create when defending themselves against attack. Even the small weasels and stoats smell strongly. The pungent, choking smells that are so characteristic of mustelids are produced

→ *Mustelids are typically small, fierce animals with long, thin bodies and short legs. Some, like the stoat (right), can be fairly large, but one, the least weasel, is the smallest carnivore on earth.*

 SEE ALSO Weasel, Least **1:**36; Marten, American **1:**48; Wolverine **1:**56; Badger, Honey **1:**82

in the anal scent glands underneath the base of the tail. The scent is used not only as a deterrent to attackers, but also to mark out territorial boundaries.

The majority of mustelids—like most other mammals—are some shade of brown. However, the family includes more species with black-and-white markings than any other group of mammals: the various types of badgers, the zorilla, the marbled polecat, and skunks, for example. A couple of northern species, such as the least weasel and stoat, may turn white in winter, and several become paler with increasing age. All mustelids have a keen sense of smell. Their hearing is excellent too, but their visual abilities are probably less well developed than in many other mammal species.

Lifestyle

Between them, the mustelids exploit a wide range of habitats, including forests, deserts, and even the sea. Most are solitary except during the mating season. Encounters between members of the same species are likely to be hostile. By contrast, the European badger lives in extended family groups known as clans. Several species of otter, as well as the spotted skunk, are relatively social animals, living in loose family groups. Most mustelids are nocturnal, but some are active any time of day or night.

Mustelids have five toes on their front and back feet, usually with a sharp claw on each. Sharp claws can be used to subdue prey or to get a good grip on tree branches. Burrowers, especially the badgers, have stouter but blunt claws. The typical slender body of most mustelids means that they are lithe and agile creatures, able to climb well and squeeze through small gaps. However, a long, thin shape also means they are less efficient than shorter-bodied mammals at preventing the loss of body heat. Although they have an unusually high metabolic rate, which compensates for heat loss by generating more, they still have to spend a lot of time hunting to acquire sufficient food to fuel their metabolism. Small weasels may need to consume half their own weight in prey every day. Mustelids are therefore always alert for something to eat. Many of them indulge in "surplus" killing when prey animals are abundant, catching more than they need and hiding the bodies away for later consumption. Badgers are bigger, and a larger body loses proportionately less heat. They become lethargic in winter, saving energy when food is in short supply. They also feed on a wider variety of food, including vegetable materials that take less energy to find than active prey.

← *These mostly southerly species of mustelid share the same body plan as the stoat and least weasel, but tend to have black, not brown, as the major coloration, or are generally larger: African striped weasel (1); zorilla (2); little grison (3); European polecat (4); Patagonian weasel (5); black-footed ferret (6); marbled polecat (7); North African banded weasel (8).*

The mink and various species of otters live in cold water and so keep themselves warm with dense, insulating fur. This has proved attractive to hunters, and many species of otter have suffered heavy losses as a result. Conversely, large numbers of the American mink have been reared on fur farms in various countries, making the species artificially numerous. Some have escaped and now cause considerable problems to the local wildlife, not least in Europe, where the native mink is being replaced by its American cousin.

Other species of mustelid have suffered a severe reduction in their numbers. For instance, the American black-footed ferret reached the brink of total extinction, but has since been successfully bred in captivity and restored to the wild. At least 16 other species of mustelid are considered to be seriously threatened. Gamekeepers and farmers have traditionally killed mustelids in defense of their livestock, exterminating several species from whole countries. Otters have proved to be highly vulnerable to pollution, dying out in parts of Europe due to the effects of acid rain and agricultural and industrial chemicals on their prey. However, many species of carnivores are now given legal protection, both nationally and internationally. Moreover, people are not as dependent on chickens or sheep for their main income as they once were and can afford to be more tolerant. Predator persecution is no longer widespread and automatic; and indeed, many species, such as badgers and otters, are very popular.

The European polecat has been domesticated to create the ferrets used in the hunting of rabbits and small game. A few mustelid species are sometimes even kept as pets.

⬆ *Spot-necked otters playfully chase a terrapin in the clear waters of Lake Tanganyika, east-central Africa. Such play reinforces social bonds and helps young otters perfect their hunting techniques.*

⬇ *Various members of the weasel family: Indian smooth-coated otter with a shell in its forepaws (1); least weasel dragging a mouse (2); American mink with a rabbit (3); European badger (4); European polecat in its winter coat (5); pine marten with a bird (6); wolverine following a scent trail (7).*

35

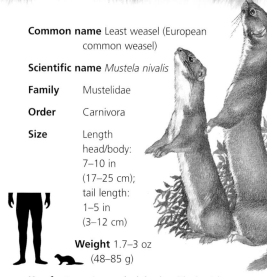

Common name Least weasel (European common weasel)

Scientific name *Mustela nivalis*

Family Mustelidae

Order Carnivora

Size Length head/body: 7–10 in (17–25 cm); tail length: 1–5 in (3–12 cm)

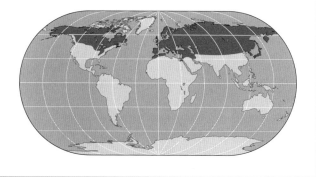

Weight 1.7–3 oz (48–85 g)

Key features Long, sleek body with short legs and short tail; flat, narrow head; fur reddish-brown in summer, with creamy-white neck and belly; turns white in winter in northern populations

Habits Solitary, territorial animals; fierce predators; very active both day and night all year round

Breeding Up to 2 litters of 1–9 young born each year after gestation period of 34–37 days. Weaned at 3–4 weeks; females sexually mature at 4 months, males at 8 months. May live up to 10 years in captivity, usually under a year in the wild

Voice Low trill to signal a friendly meeting between a male and a female; loud, harsh chirp or screech when disturbed or ready to attack

Diet Mainly small rodents, especially mice; also rabbits, lemmings, moles, pikas, birds, fish, lizards, and insects

Habitat Almost anywhere providing suitable cover and access to rodents, including meadows, farmlands, prairies, marshes, and woodlands

Distribution Northern Hemisphere: Canada, Alaska, Siberia, Japan, northern U.S., northern Europe, and Russia

Status Population: abundant. One of the more numerous small carnivores

Least Weasel

Mustela nivalis

The world's smallest carnivore, the least weasel is abundant throughout a wide area of the Northern Hemisphere. However, it is an elusive creature that is hardly ever seen, remaining well hidden in dense undergrowth most of the time.

LEAST WEASELS ARE SOLITARY, elusive creatures that are hard to see, partly because they move so fast and are gone in a flash. However, they are more common than people realize. They can easily be confused with at least two other species of weasel in North America: the long-tailed weasel (*Mustela frenata*) and the stoat, or ermine (*Mustela erminea*).

At a glance all three species look similar, but the least weasel is by far the smallest animal. The long-tailed weasel has distinct dark facial markings, and both the long-tailed weasel and the stoat have longer, bushy black-tipped tails. The European variant—the European common weasel—was once regarded as a separate species, but is now considered to be the same species as the least weasel.

World's Smallest Carnivore

Barely longer than a rat, the least weasel is the smallest carnivore in the world and the smallest of all the mustelids. It has a long, sleek body with short legs and a short tail. Its head is flat and narrow with large black eyes and prominent, rounded ears. During the summer months weasels have a reddish-brown coat with a creamy-white patch on the neck and belly. In early fall it is replaced by a lighter-colored winter coat. In some northern weasel populations, particularly in colder climates, the coat turns completely white in winter. The white color gives the animals natural camouflage against the snow and helps them avoid detection by predators.

Weasels have acute senses of sight, smell, and hearing, and often stand on their hind legs to scan their surroundings. They are incredibly

quick and agile, and often dart around erratically or bound along with their backs arched and their tails held straight out or pointing slightly upward. They have five clawed toes on each foot, which they use to grab their prey and to climb trees. Their climbing ability enables them to reach birds' nests, where they can consume both eggs and chicks. They are also strong swimmers. Weasels are powerful animals for their size and are capable of running 300 yards (275 m) while carrying a large mouse in their mouth!

Huge Appetites

Weasels are so small and dynamic and have such a fast metabolic rate that in order to survive, they must eat almost half their body weight in food each day. This means that they must catch about two mice or one fat vole per day just to stay alive. As a result, they spend a lot of time hunting, although they frequently take short rests in one of their dens.

Weasels are specialized predators of small rodents, but will also take birds, lizards, and insects whenever the opportunity arises. Their long, sleek body means that weasels are well adapted to squeezing into the smallest crevices and hunting rodents down their own burrows. In fact, the weasel's head is the widest part of its body. If it can squeeze its head into a hole, the rest of its body will follow without getting stuck. Access to such tunnels provides weasels with shelter from predators and also allows them to hunt at any time of the day or night, all year round. They do not hibernate and can hunt even under deep snow.

Weasels are renowned for being efficient killers. They catch small prey, which they kill with a few swift bites to the back of the neck. If they encounter their prey head-on in a tunnel, they kill it with a crushing bite to the windpipe. Weasels also hunt larger prey, which

⊙ *Weasels have extremely acute senses of sight, hearing, and smell. They will often stand on their hind legs to scan their surroundings.*

they stalk quietly and then pounce on the victim's back for a series of precision bites to the base of the skull. Males, which are often twice the size of females, are more likely to hunt larger prey, while the females mostly look for small rodents.

The weasel's mode of survival involves killing whatever it can, whenever it can. Faced with an abundance of mice, the voracious weasel follows the only pattern it knows and will kill more than it can eat at any one time. It sometimes stores surplus food for future meals in a side chamber off its den. Weasels are extremely versatile and can live wherever there is suitable shelter and enough food for them to reproduce successfully. They use forested, bushy, and open country, but do not normally live in wetland areas, sandy deserts, or mountainous regions. They usually make their dens in rock piles, junk heaps, abandoned buildings, and burrows dug by mice, ground squirrels, or chipmunks. In colder climates they may line their nest chambers with grass or sometimes the fur and feathers of prey.

⊕ *A weasel by a rotten log. Weasels live in a variety of habitats, including thickets and woodlands, as long as there is a good supply of suitable prey.*

No Time to Lose

Weasels only have a short life span, but they reproduce frequently and prolifically. If food supplies are high, weasels are able to take advantage of the favorable conditions, and female weasels can have up to two litters per year. The weasels usually breed from early spring to late summer, and the pregnancy lasts about five weeks. The litter size may range from as few as one or two young to as many as 20, depending on food supplies, although an average of four to six is most common.

Newborn weasels weigh about the same as an American one cent coin and are wrinkled, pink, naked, blind, and deaf. They only open their eyes after 30 days. The mother cares

diligently for her young, which develop rapidly. By seven to eight weeks the cubs begin to accompany their mother on foraging trips and can soon kill efficiently for themselves. A few weeks later the family group begins to break up, and the young start to disperse away from their mother's home range.

Weasels are heavily dependent on rodent populations. Often in the spring, when rodent populations are low, there is an associated peak in weasel mortality, probably through starvation. However, weasels also fall victim to

predators, particularly owls and martens, but also coyotes, lynx, hawks, cats, foxes, mink, and even stoats. Weasels are also frequently killed by traffic as they dash across busy highways.

Farmer's Helpers

Least weasels are often regarded as vermin by gamekeepers and poultry farmers, and have been widely hunted and trapped. They are thought to kill young game birds but are not considered so serious a threat as stoats, which can devastate fragile populations of ground-nesting birds. In fact, weasels are often killed in traps intended for stoats.

Weasels are superbly efficient at keeping in check populations of many species of rodents that can be harmful to agriculture. One female weasel will kill hundreds of mice in a year to feed herself and her offspring. Any damage to game birds or poultry is far outweighed by the weasel's value as a destroyer of pest species, which cause untold losses to growing crops and stored food. Without predators like the weasel such losses would be even greater.

⊕ *A weasel investigates a harvest mouse nest. Rodents form the bulk of the weasel's diet, and the animal is capable of crawling down burrows and squeezing into crevices in pursuit.*

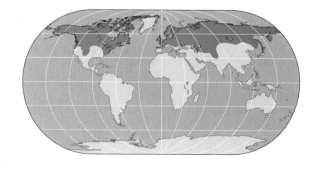

Common name
Stoat (ermine, short-tailed weasel)

Scientific name *Mustela erminea*

Family	Mustelidae
Order	Carnivora
Size	Length head/body: 7–12.5 in (17–32 cm); tail length: 1.5–5 in (4–12 cm)
	Weight 1.5–12 oz (42–340 g)
	Key features Lithe, long-bodied animal with short legs and longish, black-tipped tail; body fur rich brown with cream on belly; may turn brilliant white in winter; small head with round ears, large eyes, and long whiskers
Habits	Mainly nocturnal; terrestrial, but can swim and climb well; active and agile; a territorial, fierce, and solitary predator
Breeding	Single litter of 3–18 (usually 4–9) young born in spring after gestation period of 10 months (including delayed implantation). Weaned at 6–8 weeks; females sexually mature at 2–3 months, males at 12 months. May live up to 10 years in captivity, many fewer in the wild
Voice	Shrill squeaks when excited
Diet	Carnivorous; includes small mammals, especially rodents and rabbits; also birds and eggs, reptiles and amphibians
Habitat	Varied; from arctic tundra and moorland to forests and meadows
Distribution	Northern Hemisphere (Eurasia and North America) from within Arctic Circle to latitude 30°N
Status	Population: abundant. Common and widespread, but trapped for fur in some areas

Stoat

Mustela erminea

The stoat—or ermine, as it is called in much of its range—is the most widespread member of the mustelid family. Its range includes a wide variety of habitat from windswept arctic tundra to dense forest.

THE STOAT ALMOST CERTAINLY EVOLVED as a rodent-catching specialist, but its physical adaptations and hunting techniques make it almost equally effective in pursuit of other vertebrate prey. The animal's sinuous body is slim enough to follow rats and rabbits into burrows and to turn around inside a tunnel. Its spine is flexible, which allows it to travel much faster than its short legs might suggest. A stoat can streak through long grass at amazing speeds, take sudden leaps and bounds, and change direction in an instant. It can also climb trees and rocks and swim extremely well. Stoats have been found up to 50 feet (15 m) in trees and over half a mile (800 m) offshore in lakes. They have crossed even larger expanses of water, apparently unaided, to colonize small coastal islands in parts of their range. Stoats are light enough to run along the surface of fresh snow, but can also move below the surface, out of sight of predators and sheltered from the wind.

Regional Differences
There are as many as 29 recognized subspecies of stoat, most of them from North America, where they are often known as short-tailed weasels. They are distinguished as much by geography as by any obvious physical characteristics. As a general rule, American stoats are smaller than those in the Old World, and throughout the stoat's geographical range males are bigger than females, sometimes twice the size. Perhaps the most notable regional difference is that in higher latitudes stoats turn white in winter, while those in more temperate zones retain their brown color all year round.

Stoats are small, but they sometimes use surprisingly large home ranges. An active male

⊕ *Stoats carry out all their explorations at high speed and not surprisingly burn up a great deal of energy. The long, thin body is also inefficient when it comes to conserving heat.*

 SEE ALSO Weasel, Least **1**:36; Fox, Arctic **2**:70; Bear Family, The **2**:82

will usually occupy a range of between 50 and 150 acres (20 and 60 ha), although ranges up to 500 acres (200 ha) have been recorded. Male ranges overlap partially with those of females, which are usually about half the size of the area used by males. Within their ranges both males and females maintain an area of private territory, inside which other stoats are not tolerated. Territories are marked out with scent and droppings placed on landmarks such as rocks and tree stumps. The resident stoat will regularly patrol its home area. Hunting and patrolling normally take place between dusk and dawn, and a stoat may cover anything up to 10 miles (16 km) a night. Both males and females use dens for sleeping during the day—there are usually several within the home range, located in rock crevices or rodent burrows.

⊖ *A stoat emerges from the shelter of a log. Scent and droppings are deposited on logs and rocks by both males and females to mark out a home range.*

Frenetic Activity

A stoat's heart beats up to 500 times a minute, and almost all activities are carried out at a similarly frenetic pace. Stoats are incredibly inquisitive and will investigate any nook or cranny within their range, darting in and out of burrows, tree holes, and crevices, nose twitching and ears pricked for the scent or sound of potential prey.

Stoats have excellent eyesight, but in the darkness underground they rely heavily on their long, sensitive whiskers to find their way around. Stoats do not hibernate, so they have to remain active and well fed right through the winter. Where possible, a stoat will make provision for the cold season by hiding caches (stores) of spare meat caught earlier in the year. The fact that stoats will kill more than they can eat means they are sometimes accused of killing for fun, when in fact they may be just thinking ahead. Given the chance, all the excess will be carefully stockpiled for later.

Polygamous Relationships

Male stoats are larger than females, and as such are sometimes at a disadvantage when hunting because they cannot pursue small prey such as mice and voles into such tight spaces. However, large size comes into its own when defending a territory, within which the resident male will have by far the best chances of mating with all the local females. Once mating is over, the male moves on almost immediately in search of another female and plays no further part in the rearing of his future family. In fact, stoat pregnancy is so long that more often than not the father will be dead by the time his kits are born, some 10 months after mating. Like many other mustelids, stoat gestation includes a nine-month period of delayed implantation, during which embryonic development is halted at an early stage. Development resumes the following spring, and

Winter White

All stoats undergo two molts each year, in the spring and fall. The timing of the molt is determined by the changing day length. For example, in the fall the change to a winter coat is triggered when the daylight hours drop below a critical limit. Hence the molt happens sooner in the north, where the winter days are shorter. While molting is controlled by day length, the color of the winter coat is determined by air temperature. However short the days, if the average temperature remains above a certain level, the new winter coat will be brown. Below that temperature it will be white, providing the stoat with useful camouflage in a climate where snow is likely. In areas where the temperature fluctuates around the threshold level, the coat will be a mixture of brown and white. The molt from a summer to winter coat begins on the belly and moves forward to the head. In spring the process happens in reverse.

In the most northerly parts of its range the stoat's winter pelt is highly prized for its fineness and purity of color. Despite being trapped for their fur, stoats are among the world's most successful predatory species.

⟲ *A stoat uses its keen sense of hearing and smell to detect prey. Its sinuous body allows it to pursue rats and rabbits into their burrows and to turn around in tight spaces with ease.*

litters of up to 13 babies are born. They are tiny, blind, and virtually naked, apart from a fine covering of wispy white hairs. The family is raised in a den lined with the fur and feathers of prey animals, and defended fiercely by the mother. If she is disturbed, she will often move the family to a new, safe place, carrying them one at a time in her mouth.

The young develop quickly. By six weeks they are as heavy as their mother and begin to accompany her on hunting excursions. She teaches them the necessary techniques and

gives them dead or maimed prey animals to practice on. Stoats are unusual in that they will kill animals larger than themselves without help from other members of their species.

Stoats are among several European animals to have been introduced to New Zealand by settlers. By the early 19th century New Zealand already had a serious problem with introduced mammals, especially rabbits. Such animals had been taken there some years before to provide meat, fur, and sport hunting. As in Australia, the New Zealand rabbit population rapidly grew out of control, and the introduction of stoats was a misguided attempt to curb their numbers. Although stoats did kill rabbits, the whole operation was a disaster. The stoats soon found that it was much easier to kill New Zealand's native birds, which—in the absence of native mammalian predators—had no instinctive fear of the stoat and in many cases were flightless. By the turn of the century stoats had overrun both North and South Islands. They remain widespread even today despite rigorous attempts to control them.

Polecat

Mustela putorius

Common name Polecat

Scientific name *Mustela putorius*

Family Mustelidae

Order Carnivora

Size Length head/body: 12–18 in (30–46 cm); tail length: 5–6 in (12–14 cm). Male generally larger than female

Weight 1–3 lb (0.5–1.4 kg)

Key features Resembles short-legged cat, with a long, sinuous body; almost black in summer, but pale cream in winter; bold, dark mask pattern on face throughout the year

Habits Mainly nocturnal; solitary; forages along the ground; occasionally climbs

Breeding One litter per year of 3–7 (can be up to 12) young born about June after gestation period of 42 days. Weaned at 1 month; sexually mature at 1 year. May live up to 14 years in captivity, 5 in the wild

Voice May squeak and hiss occasionally, but sound is not used for social communication

Diet Mainly rabbits and voles; also birds, frogs, occasionally eels caught in wet grass; whatever is most abundant and easiest to catch

Habitat Young forestry plantations and woodland, but mainly on farmland where there is plenty of cover in hedges, walls, and old buildings

Distribution Western Europe from Britain and Spain east to the Black Sea and Baltic countries

Status Population: abundant. Previously eradicated from Scotland and most of England, but now recolonizing, thanks to reduced persecution

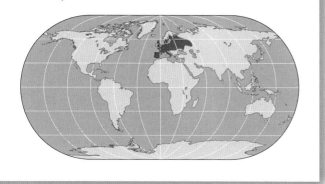

Polecats were persecuted relentlessly in the past as a means of protecting gamebirds and chicken houses from predation. However, present populations are expanding in many areas.

POLECATS WERE OFTEN TRAPPED FOR their fine fur, which was highly prized by the European nobility in medieval times. They also had a reputation for being bloodthirsty killers and were therefore believed to be a threat to livestock, especially chickens. In 16th-century England they were declared vermin by Queen Elizabeth I, and many thousands were killed. Later, large numbers were trapped by gamekeepers, especially in the 19th century.

Polecats are particularly vulnerable to traps, especially the old leghold traps used to catch rabbits. The traps were often set in rabbit holes or gaps in hedges and walls, exactly where polecats dive in and out searching for prey. Such traps were sometimes deliberately used to catch polecats, but many more polecats were killed as a result of accidental trapping.

Respite from Persecution

Although polecats were once widespread and abundant, numbers decreased sharply. However, the First World War brought a welcome reprieve from the activities of gamekeepers in Britain and elsewhere, and soon polecat populations began to increase. Enough polecats had survived in remote areas to begin recolonizing parts of Wales and England, but the species was already extinct in Scotland.

Polecats are not much affected by diseases and parasites, but often fall victim to poisoning, usually as a result of eating poisoned rats. Modern rat poisons are very powerful, and many polecats live around farmyards where rat poisoning is routine practice. Another modern threat comes from road traffic. Whole families may be annihilated as they play in the road or attempt to cross it. However, it appears that new forestry plantations provide excellent polecat habitat, especially where young trees and grass provide shelter for huge populations of voles, a favorite food. Further assistance has come from the recovery of rabbits after the disease myxomatosis devastated populations in Britain in the 1950s.

The ferret, a domesticated form of the polecat, has been bred in captivity from as early as the 4th century B.C. It was initially raised to assist with hunting, but is now a familiar household pet, especially in the United States.

Ambush Techniques

Across Europe polecats seem to be a lowland species. However, urban areas and huge, open arable fields with little cover and few prey animals are uninviting habitats. Polecats have acute hearing and good night vision. They hunt mainly after dark, spending about four hours every night searching for food, mainly ambushing rabbits and voles. Polecats will also eat eggs, small birds, frogs, and the occasional eel found wriggling in wet grass. The animals usually amble around in an unhurried manner, pausing to investigate interesting sounds and smells, but they can also move rapidly with a bounding gait and with the back arched high.

Polecats are playful creatures, but normally live alone, each occupying a home range of about 250 acres (100 ha), within which they may use five or more different dens.

Polecats can produce a pungent scent from large scent glands. The scent is used to mark stones and logs within their territory and probably helps the animals recognize each other. The scent glands also provide some protection: Few animals will try to attack polecats because of their strong smell.

⊖ Polecats have luxurious fur that is dark colored in winter, but pale cream in the summer. Their faces have a mask pattern all year round.

Common name Black-footed ferret

Scientific name *Mustela nigripes*

Family Mustelidae

Order Carnivora

Size Length head/body: 14–18 in (36–45 cm); tail length: 5–6 in (12–15 cm). Male generally about 10% bigger than female

Weight 2–2.4 lb (0.9–1.1 kg)

Key features Slender animal the size of a small cat; pale yellow with short black legs, black mask, and tail tip

Habits Usually nocturnal; spends the day underground

Breeding One litter of up to 6 (usually 3–4) young born March–April after gestation period of 45 days. Weaned at 1 month; sexually mature at 1 year. May live 12 years in captivity, similar in the wild

Voice Normally silent

Diet Mostly small rodents, especially prairie dogs

Habitat Grasslands

Distribution Formerly widespread in the American Midwest from Texas to Canadian border; now survives only as reintroduced populations in Montana, South Dakota, and Wyoming

Status Population: about 500, mostly in captivity; CITES I since 1975

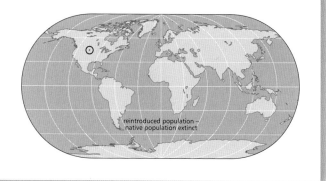

reintroduced population – native population extinct

Black-Footed Ferret

Mustela nigripes

The black-footed ferret specialized in hunting prairie dogs and suffered heavily when these animals were eliminated from agricultural areas. The ferrets have been reintroduced to the wild from captive-bred stock, but its future is precarious.

BLACK-FOOTED FERRETS WERE NEVER common. They lived alone and were often spaced apart by more than 3.5 miles (6 km). They used to be found widely across the American short-grass prairies from Texas to beyond the Canadian border. Over 90 percent of the ferrets' food was prairie dogs, but the animals would also kill mice and other small prey. A single ferret could get by on what it could catch in quite a small prairie dog colony (called a town), living as a "predator in residence."

Disappearing Food Source

The black-footed ferret's reliance on prairie dogs for food and shelter has contributed to its precarious situation in the wild. During the 20th century whole prairie dog towns were plowed over or eliminated using traps, gassing, and poisons to make way for agriculture and ranching. Growing crops successfully among the prairie dogs was impractical, and farmers found their tractors often got stuck in collapsed burrows. Prairie dog towns were also a serious hazard for horses and their riders, with many broken legs and other injuries resulting from tripping over dirt mounds and tunnel entrances. In Kansas—a former stronghold of prairie dogs—over 98 percent of the towns were eliminated in fewer than 100 years.

As a result of the demise of the prairie dog, ferret numbers also dwindled, and the species was believed to have become extinct. Sightings of ferrets and their tracks were reported from time to time, and a small population was discovered in South Dakota, but it had died out

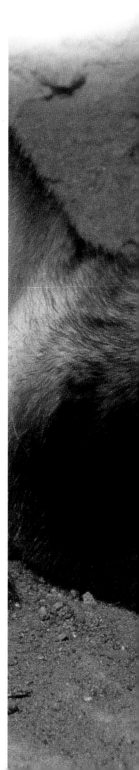

SEE ALSO Polecat 1:44; Prairie Dog, Black-Tailed 7:56

⊕ Black-footed ferrets commonly inhabit the burrows of prairie dogs (rodents of the squirrel family), taking over part of the tunnel system as predator in residence.

by 1974. In 1981 a substantial wild population of black-footed ferrets was found on a ranch in Wyoming. Detailed studies of the animals began, but the white-tailed prairie dogs on which they mainly fed were hit by disease and suffered catastrophic losses. The ferrets themselves caught canine distemper and died out. By 1987 there were none left in the wild.

Meanwhile, a few ferrets had been taken into captivity to form an insurance against total extinction. Their numbers slowly built up, and by the end of 1991 there were over 300, enough for the United States Fish and Wildlife Service to begin releasing some back into the wild. Over several years a few hundred were restored to Montana and South Dakota. They began to breed, although rather slowly; but many died, and the black-footed ferret is still not securely reestablished on the prairies.

While reintroduced wild populations were suffering setbacks, numbers of black-footed ferrets in captivity continued to increase. By 1996 there were more than 400 in captivity, and today the animals are kept in many zoos and wildlife conservation centers.

The black-footed ferret now enjoys legal protection, and prairie dogs are no longer massacred. The current problem challenging conservationists is that the entire population of black-footed ferrets comes from only a few animals removed from Wyoming in the 1980s. The population has inevitably become inbred, resulting in limited breeding success and poor survival of offspring. It remains to be seen whether the newly restored populations will manage to overcome this problem and increase to form a viable wild population. Even if they do, it is unlikely that black-footed ferrets will ever again be widespread, because prairie dogs—on whom their existence relies—have long since disappeared from huge areas of the Midwest.

Widely Dispersed

Black-footed ferrets have litters of up to six offspring in the spring. The young emerge from underground in early July, having grown almost as large as their mother. The family stays together until the fall, when the young males disperse. Young females often stay nearby. Adult males do not live with their family or help raise them. Black-footed ferrets need to be widely dispersed to avoid too many animals trying to feed off prairie dogs in any one place.

Common name American marten
(American pine
marten, American sable)

Scientific name *Martes americana*

Family   Mustelidae

Order   Carnivora

Size   Length head/body: 20–27 in (50–68 cm); tail
length: 7–9 in (18–23 cm)

Weight 10–44 oz (280–1,250 g). Male
generally at least a third bigger
than female

Key features Slender cat-sized animal with short legs
and bushy tail; fur ranges from pale brown to
almost black with an orange or yellowish
throat patch

Habits   Active throughout the year and also at any
time of day or night; climbs well

Breeding   Up to 5 (usually 3) young born once a year in
the spring after gestation period of 1 month.
Weaned at 6 weeks; sexually mature at
15–24 months. May live 17 years in captivity,
at least 15 in the wild

Voice   Normally silent; sometimes makes chuckling
noises or gives the occasional scream

Diet   Wide variety of small animals; also insects,
fruit, and seeds

Habitat   Deciduous and coniferous forests

Distribution From Alaska eastward to eastern Canada;
also Rocky Mountains and Sierra Nevada

Status   Population: abundant. Widespread but
elusive; rare and declining in some places

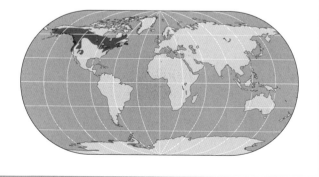

American Marten

Martes americana

A charismatic small forest predator, the American marten has suffered heavily from the activities of trappers and also from habitat loss.

AMERICAN MARTENS ARE TYPICALLY associated with northern forests, particularly those dominated by mature spruce and fir trees. They also occur in deciduous forests, but the most distinctive features of their habitat are the complex mixture of different species, the different ages of the trees, and the presence of glades and clearings. Such habitat generally has abundant and diverse prey. The martens will move around using different areas at different times of year, depending on food availability.

Disappearing Habitats

Martens are found across much of North America from Alaska through the forested parts of Canada and east into the eastern United States. At one time they were also fairly common in the southeastern United States. However, the harvesting of trees and clearing of forests to make way for farmland have since deprived the animals of enormous areas of suitable habitat. Moreover, the dense and lustrous fur of the marten made it a prime target for fur trappers, and the animals were easy to catch. As a result, martens were eliminated from the southern part of their natural range and have become quite rare in many other parts of their range, too.

American martens do not hibernate and are active throughout the year. They hunt mainly on the ground, although they can also climb well. They are perfectly capable of swimming, but do not enter the water unless absolutely necessary, preferring to cross streams by way of overhanging trees and logs.

American martens have a very varied diet, and more than 100 different types of food have substances—precisely to deter animals such as martens. However, the American marten is not wholly carnivorous and will also eat large quantities of fruit in the fall and even ripe seeds. The indigestible remains of its varied diet can be seen as chewed fragments in its shiny black feces, which are often deposited on open tracks and prominent logs, probably to help mark out its territory.

Martens are extremely active creatures and can move rapidly when they need to. They trot and bound around, stopping frequently to investigate likely places to find food. Most of their foraging is done early in the day and late in the evening, although martens may be active at any time of the day or night.

Delayed Implantation

Martens are territorial, and each one lives alone, except during the breeding season. A male may live with a chosen female for a couple of weeks in the summer, during which time the animals will play together and indulge in mock fights. They mate many times, often with several partners in a season. The pregnancy lasts only a month, but births in midwinter are avoided by a process known as delayed implantation. The fertilized egg remains dormant for over 200 days before implanting itself in the wall of the uterus and developing normally. As a result, the young are not born until the following April, when there is plenty of food, and the weather is less challenging.

Litters average three young, but sometimes there are as many as five babies in the family. The offspring are born in a den among boulders, a hollow tree, or the shelter of a fallen log. They grow rapidly, and by midsummer they are almost as large as their mother. Males will grow to at least one-third bigger than females. The young face few predators and are nimble enough to escape likely attackers. However, winter is a difficult time when it is hard to find mammal prey under deep snow. Nevertheless, survival rates are high, and some martens live for up to 15 years.

⊖ *The American marten is becoming quite rare in places as a result of the loss of its forest habitat to farming and logging.*

been reported. Their main prey consists of small mammals such as red-backed voles. However, they will also eat mice and occasionally larger animals, such as chipmunks, ground squirrels, pocket gophers, and even snowshoe hares. Their preference for voles and mice is due to the fact that such prey is common and easy to catch in the long grass of forest clearings. Martens will also eat birds if they can catch them and any large-bodied insects, except those that produce evil-tasting

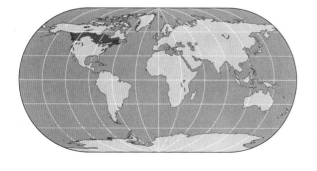

Common name Fisher

Scientific name *Martes pennanti*

Family	Mustelidae
Order	Carnivora
Size	Length head/body: 18.5–29.5 in (47–75 cm); tail length: 12–16.5 in (30–42 cm)
Weight	Male 7.7–12 lb (3.5–5.5 kg), occasionally up to 19.8 lb (9 kg); female 4.4–5.5 lb (2–2.5 kg)
Key features	Cat-sized weasel with short legs, long body, and long, bushy tail; head is wedge shaped, relatively large, rounded ears; coat is dark and varies between sexes, seasons, and individuals
Habits	Active any time of day in short bouts of 2–5 hours; territorial and mainly solitary, only meeting during the mating season; mainly ground dwelling, but climbs trees with ease
Breeding	One litter per year of 1–5 pups born in spring after gestation period of 352 days (including an uncertain period of delayed implantation). Weaned at 2–4 months; females sexually mature at 1 year, males at 2 years. May live for 10 years in captivity, similar in the wild
Voice	Growls, hissing coughs, or clicks, but normally silent
Diet	Porcupines, snowshoe hares, and small rodents; also carrion, birds, eggs, insects, reptiles, and amphibians; some fruit and nuts
Habitat	Mature forest and swampy woodlands
Distribution	Northern U.S. and Canada; distribution extends south in mountainous regions
Status	Population: unknown, perhaps tens of thousands. Protected in some U.S. states

Fisher

Martes pennanti

The fisher is a large marten. It is an opportunistic predator and one of the few animals that hunts porcupines. However, trapping for the fur trade has eradicated it from many parts of the United States.

FISHERS ARE MEDIUM-SIZED MAMMALS and the largest of the martens. They are shy, elusive creatures and are rarely seen alive in the wild. Contrary to their name, fishers do not eat fish. They were probably named by American settlers who noticed their similarity to European polecats, which are also known as fitches or fitch ferrets. Fishers are sometimes called American sable because of their luxuriant fur.

Fishers are generalized predators, which means they will eat any animal they can catch. They are among the few animals that will eat porcupines. Their diet makes them popular with foresters, since porcupines can damage or even kill young trees by removing their bark. Fishers also eat the flesh of large dead animals, such as deer and moose.

Porcupine Hunt

When hunting porcupines, a fisher travels long distances on familiar routes, inspecting most of the porcupine dens along the way. If it encounters a porcupine, there is usually a long, drawn out attack that can last over half an hour. Porcupines are usually attacked on the ground. If one is up a tree, the fisher will climb up and try to force it to the end of a branch. If the porcupine falls to the ground, it is open to attack. The fisher circles the porcupine, attempting to bite its face. The porcupine tries to keep its back toward the fisher and its face close to a tree trunk. When it can, the porcupine charges backward, flailing its spiny tail. During such charges it exposes its face, which has no protective quills, and the fisher attacks repeatedly. Eventually, when the porcupine is exhausted, the fisher flips it over and attacks the soft, unprotected underbelly. All

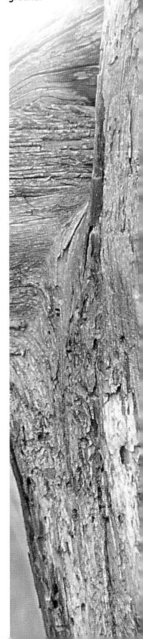

⊖ *Fishers are excellent climbers and even hunt some of their prey in the branches of trees. They will kill tree porcupines by knocking them off the end of a branch and attacking them on the ground.*

other prey is killed with a quick bite to the back of the neck. The fisher consumes the porcupine from the belly, eating the heart, lungs, and liver, and leaving the skin, large bones, feet, and intestines. During attacks on porcupines fishers frequently get quills stuck in their body. They do not seem to cause serious discomfort, but can be lethal if they puncture a vital organ.

Fishers travel fairly long distances when hunting and use temporary dens for resting, particularly when progress is made difficult by heavy snowfall. Dens are usually under logs, brush piles, or tree roots, in hollow trees or ground burrows, or under snow. They are rarely used for more than two or three days.

Fishers are territorial and, like many mustelids, mark their home ranges with urine and scent from anal, cheek, abdominal, neck, flank, and feet glands. Scent marking is also used to communicate during the breeding season, when males will travel long distances to find receptive females. Males and females only come together briefly for breeding, and the males do not stay to help rear the family. Young are born in spring in nursing dens that are usually well concealed high in hollow trees or on rocky ledges. Although blind and helpless at birth, they grow quickly. They can kill their own prey after four months and are fully independent by their first winter.

Threats to Survival

Threatened by the fur trade and logging, fishers have been eradicated from many parts of their original range, particularly along the western coastal parts of the United States. Their persecution was at its most severe in the early to mid-1900s owing to the fashion for furs, but still continues today. The black, silky pelts of the females are particularly valuable.

Because they will eat carrion, fishers are easy to bait and trap. They are still hunted legally in some states. In others they are listed as threatened and given protection. Fishers are also suffering from the effects of deforestation. Many of the old-growth forests in which they like to make their nursing dens are being cut down for timber and other commercial uses. Fishers dislike crossing open areas and so are vulnerable if the forests they inhabit become broken into small patches.

Common name American mink

Scientific name *Mustela vison*

Family	Mustelidae
Order	Carnivora
Size	Length head/body: 12–18.5 in (30–47 cm); tail length: 5–9 in (13–23 cm)
Weight	1.9–4 lb (0.9–1.8 kg); female 1–1.8 lb (0.5–0.8 kg)
Key features	Resembles short-legged, glossy black or dark-brown cat; pointed muzzle
Habits	Mainly nocturnal; swims and dives; uses burrows and lairs among tree roots at water's edge, also rabbit burrows, but does not dig for itself
Breeding	One litter of 4–6 young born April–May after gestation period of 39–78 days, including a variable period of delayed implantation. Weaned at 5–6 weeks; sexually mature at 2 years. May live for 10 years in captivity, 2–3 in the wild
Voice	Hisses when threatened; may scream defiantly in self-defense, but usually silent
Diet	Fish, frogs, small mammals, waterside birds and their eggs; also some invertebrates such as beetles and worms, especially along coasts
Habitat	Mostly lowland areas beside rivers, lakes, and ponds; also marshland and along seashores
Distribution	Canada; eastern and most of central U.S.; introduced to Europe: in Britain, France, Italy, Spain, Ireland, Scandinavia, and Iceland
Status	Population: abundant. Increasing in Europe

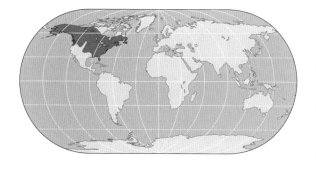

American Mink

Mustela vison

A widespread waterside predator in North America, the American mink has also become established in parts of Europe, where it is proving a successful but unwelcome invader.

AMERICAN MINK ARE WIDESPREAD and fairly common across most of North America. They are substantially smaller than otters and much darker in color, appearing almost black, especially when wet. Their droppings are easily recognized, being black and cylindrical and about the diameter of a pencil. They are deposited on rocks and logs at the water's edge and smell distinctly unpleasant.

Mink are usually associated with slow-flowing rivers and lowland lakes, preferring places where there is plenty of overhanging bankside vegetation. Each has a hunting territory of about half a mile of riverbank or lakeshore. Mink are less common in upland areas, but in some places they have established colonies along the coast. Here they can reach high densities, as many as three individuals per mile (1.6 km) of coastline. Along the seashore mink behave rather like coastal otters, feeding on rockpool fish, but also climbing steep grassy cliff slopes to raid gulls' nests.

Lone Rangers

Mink are active at dusk and after dark, bounding around on land and swimming and diving underwater. They are unsociable creatures, and each one tends to live in its own territory. Male territories do not overlap, but often include parts of the territories of one or more females. In spring some of the males set out on long journeys in search of females and may travel widely across the countryside, helping colonize new areas. However, even after finding a mate mink still do not set up families. There is no pair bond, and after mating the animals live apart. Females produce only one litter each year, usually in April or May. The average litter size is four to six young, although captive mink can produce many more. The babies spend up to two months in their mother's nest, normally in a burrow or among dense tree roots. They are weaned at about five to six weeks, and the family disperses soon afterward. The babies grow rapidly to reach adult size before the end of the year and are capable of breeding the following spring. Females can still breed at seven years, although few reach this age in the wild, and most mink die within the first three years of life.

Dangers Faced

Young mink tend to disperse away from their mother's territory, sometimes traveling more than 6 miles (10 km) in their search for a place to live. Once they have established a new territory, mink tend to stay in the same place, often for several years. They need to know their home patch well, since they are in constant danger from gamekeepers, farmers, and trappers. Thousands are killed each year. Others may drown in traps set to catch fish. On the other hand, mink have little to fear from natural predators and are well able to defend themselves if attacked by foxes or cats. Perhaps that is why they are often active in broad daylight, although their main activity takes place after dark, when prey animals are more likely to be found.

Mink eat fish and birds, but also take beetles, worms, and other invertebrates. Most of their prey consists of small creatures, but often mink will attack rabbits. In fact, they will eat almost anything apart from fruit and other plant material. Mink are such successful hunters they spend less than 20 percent of their time away from the den. The rest of the time they are safely tucked away asleep or grooming their

Mink are solitary creatures and only meet to breed. However, after breeding, they do not set up families, and the female raises the young alone.

produced, ranging from silver-white to cream, as well as the natural dark chocolate-brown.

The mink industry expanded in Britain and Europe during the 1950s, producing more than a quarter of a million skins per year. But the mink is able to climb and squeeze through small gaps, and inevitably many escaped. The animals often proved adaptable and survived successfully in the wild, despite attempts to eradicate them. Mink spread widely and within 30 years occupied most of Britain. They were also found over most of Iceland, Norway, and Sweden. Today they continue to spread eastward in mainland Europe and are now also established in Ireland.

Invaders of Europe

The American mink's extraordinarily successful invasion has added another species to the mammals of Europe, but its spread has been accompanied by serious losses of native animals. The rare European mink (*Mustela lutreola*) has now become almost extinct, and in Britain the water vole has disappeared from nearly 90 percent of sites where it was formerly common. Mink are good swimmers and have managed to reach islands over 2 miles (3 km) offshore where seabirds had previously nested in safety, protected by the surrounding water. Here they have killed hundreds of adult birds and chicks, as well as eating the eggs. Whole colonies have been wiped out in the space of only a few breeding seasons, and in some places seabirds have been almost eliminated.

When mink get into parks with captive ducks (often pinioned so they cannot fly), they cause mayhem, killing many birds. They also create havoc on chicken farms and fish farms where there are high densities of juicy trout to eat. Gamekeepers regard mink as vermin because they take many gamebird chicks and eggs. However, recent studies suggest that mink numbers may be falling in Britain as otters recolonize rivers, perhaps displacing the smaller mink. In the United States mink seem less of a problem, so perhaps one day they will achieve a better balance with nature in Europe, too.

sleek and lustrous fur. The den may be in an old rabbit burrow among rocks or piles of brushwood, but it is always close to the water's edge. It may sometimes have a separate entrance underwater. Each mink may use several dens at different times of the year. Mink do not hibernate, although they become significantly less active during winter months.

Fur Farming

Mink have a glossy coat that has been highly prized by the fashion industry. Although wild mink are easy to catch, trappers could not obtain enough skins to meet demand. As a result, special mink farms were established, especially in Europe. Mink were first imported from America to European fur farms in the 1920s, but only small numbers were kept until after the Second World War. However, in the postwar years raising mink for the fur trade was seen as a lucrative new moneymaker. The animals bred well in captivity and could be fed cheaply on unwanted animal waste, including bits of chicken from the expanding broiler fowl industry. Moreover, through careful selective breeding even more valuable colored furs were

⊕ *A fur farm in Estonia. Breeding mink for the fur trade was once a lucrative business, and a mink coat was considered the height of luxury. However, fur has since fallen out of fashion.*

The Price of Freedom

In 1998 animal rights supporters broke into British fur farms and released thousands of mink. Whether fur farming is right or wrong, it was an irresponsible act, widely condemned by conservationists and animal welfare groups. The released mink posed a serious threat to many other species, and such releases were also cruel to the mink themselves, since they had been bred in captivity for many generations: Like pet mice or guinea pigs, they were unaccustomed to life in the wild. Large numbers were easily recaptured, since they had no idea how to avoid being caught. Many were also run over on the roads. Others were killed by dogs or shot by annoyed landowners and gamekeepers. Some mink even found their way into people's houses, having been driven by hunger to enter through the cat flap in search of food.

Fashions have changed, and fur coats are no longer so much in demand. Mink farming is less profitable today than it once was, and animal welfare legislation imposes many conditions on the managers of fur farms. Large numbers of businesses have closed down, leaving fewer mink in captivity. However, populations of wild American mink in Europe continue to prosper and are likely to remain permanently established there.

⊙ *An American mink returns to a henhouse in Britain to feed on hens it killed the previous night. Mink have also been responsible for losses to many native animals.*

European Mink

The native European mink *(Mustela lutreola)* is similar in appearance to its American cousin, but has a white area around its upper lip. European mink prefer to live beside fast-flowing water rather than lakes and coast, but have become notably scarce in recent times. The species is now found only in small areas of France, Spain, Estonia, and Romania, having been driven out of the rest of Europe by habitat loss and the invading American mink. It has disappeared from about 80 percent of its former range and is still in decline. Urgent efforts are being made to establish captive-breeding colonies from which the species might one day be restored to the wild.

The rare European mink (above) has a white patch around its upper lip.

Common name Wolverine (glutton, skunk bear)

Scientific name *Gulo gulo*

Family   Mustelidae

Order   Carnivora

Size   Length head/body: 24–26 in (62–67 cm); tail length: 5–10 in (13–25 cm); height at shoulder: 14–17 in (35–43 cm)

Weight 20–65 lb (9–29 kg). Male at least 10% bigger than female

Key features Low, thickset animal with short legs and large, powerful paws; coat dark brown but paler on face and flanks; tail thick and bushy

Habits   Solitary creature that roams widely; mainly nocturnal in summer

Breeding   One litter of up to 4 babies born February–March after gestation period of 30–40 days (including up to 9 months delayed implantation). Weaned at 8–10 weeks; sexually mature at 2–3 years. May live up to 18 years in captivity, 11 in the wild

Voice   Hisses and growls when annoyed; also playful squeaks and grunts

Diet   Mostly rodents; sometimes larger mammals, especially as carrion; also fruit, berries, birds, and eggs

Habitat   Mountainous forests, rocky areas, and tundra in summer

Distribution Widely distributed across northern Europe and Russia; also Canada and northern U.S.

Status   Population: unknown, probably low thousands; IUCN Vulnerable

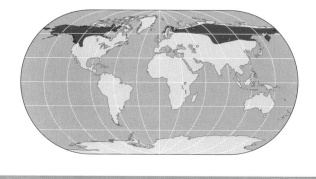

Wolverine

Gulo gulo

A naturally scarce animal, the wolverine has a reputation as a fierce and greedy predator. Ruthless persecution has resulted in it becoming quite rare.

WOLVERINES ARE FOUND AROUND the edges of the Arctic, in both North America and Europe. The cold conditions and long winters mean that plants grow slowly, and prey animals are scarce. As a result, animals that live in the Arctic all year—particularly predators like the wolverine—tend to be low in number. Wolverines need huge areas to provide them with enough food. They must wander widely to feed, sometimes covering over 30 miles (48 km) in a day. Often there is only one wolverine in more than 200 square miles (500 sq. km).

The summer months may be spent out on open tundra or mountainsides, but come the winter wolverines will migrate to the shelter of forests, sometimes journeying up to 50 miles (80 km). Although they can cope with deep snow, if there is too much of it, the short-legged wolverines have difficulty chasing and capturing prey. As a result, winter is normally spent in the relative shelter of conifer forests, where the snow is usually less deep.

Waste Not, Want Not

Although wolverines normally prey on small creatures, such as Arctic hares and lemmings, they must make the most of any food they manage to find. In the fall there are plenty of ripe berries to eat and many inexperienced young mammals and birds that are easy to kill. During leaner times the wolverine will sometimes attack animals as large as deer and wild sheep, storing surplus food for later. (The wolverine's powerful jaws mean it can drag down animals much larger than itself.) The wolverine's tendency to kill more than it needs has given rise to its reputation as a wanton killer. There are many folktales about the cunning and bloodthirstiness of wolverines. Fur

① Not unlike a small bear in appearance, the wolverine is the largest member of the weasel family. It is territorial and will defend its home patch against others of the same sex.

trappers complain that the animals steal from their traps, and reindeer herdsmen fear that wolverines will attack their animals.

Wolverines mate in the summer and would normally give birth after a few weeks. However, they avoid producing young in midwinter by a process known as delayed implantation. As a result, the babies are not born until about April, just in time for the long days and relatively abundant food supplies of the Arctic summer. The young continue to use the mother's den until May. They stay within her normal home range until about August. After that they tend to disperse, especially the males.

The Human Threat

Many wolverines are shot on sight, not just because of the damage they might cause, but also for their fur. Their long hairs tend not to freeze together in the intense cold of the Arctic, so the pelts are prized by local people for trimming the hoods of winter coats.

Wolverines are sensitive creatures and easily disturbed. The remote areas in which they once lived in safety are becoming more accessible. The remaining populations of wolverines are regarded as threatened, and the species seems likely to suffer further decline. Wolverines were at one time found much farther south in Europe than they are today, even into Germany. In the United States they used to occur across the whole continent as far south as Arizona and New Mexico. Today they are extinct east of Montana, with a few remaining in California and Idaho.

Wolverines are still widespread in Canada, and British Columbia is a stronghold with about 5,000 animals. Little is known about numbers in Russia and Siberia, but in northern Scandinavia wolverines have become rare and now occur mainly in the remote mountains of Norway and Sweden. It is thought that only 40 are left in the whole of Finland.

⊕ *The wolverine's broad feet allow it to run on snow without sinking in.*

Common name
European otter

Scientific name *Lutra lutra*

Family Mustelidae

Order Carnivora

Size Length head/body: 24–35 in (60–90 cm); tail length: 14–18.5 in (35–47 cm); height at shoulder: about 6 in (15 cm). Male about 20% bigger than female

Weight 13–37 lb (6–17 kg)

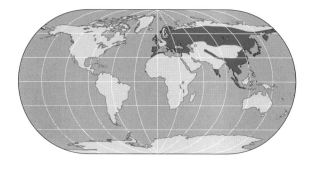

Key features Long, slender body with short legs and long, tapering tail; light- or dark-brown fur with broad, flattened head, small ears, and small eyes; all 4 feet are webbed

Habits Lives alone; swims and dives well but can be active on land; usually nocturnal, but may come out during the day

Breeding Usually 2–3 cubs born after gestation period of 2 months; births at any time of year in western Europe, more seasonal in the north and east. Weaned at 4 months; sexually mature at 1 year. May live up to 15 years in captivity, about 3–4 in the wild

Voice Occasional shrill whistle, otherwise silent

Diet Slow-swimming fish, especially eels, but also mussels, shrimps, crabs, and lobsters

Habitat Edges of rivers and lakes, often in reed beds; rocky coasts in some areas

Distribution From Britain throughout most of western Europe east to China and Japan; also in south India, Sri Lanka, Malaysia, Sumatra, and parts of North Africa

Status Population: widespread but scarce; IUCN Vulnerable; CITES I. Declining in most areas; has become extinct in parts of Europe in the last 50 years

European Otter *Lutra lutra*

European otters are popular creatures. However, few people have ever seen one or are likely to do so, since they are becoming increasingly rare as a result of urbanization and pollution.

THE EUROPEAN OTTER IS A MEMBER of the weasel family and has a typical long, thin body with short legs. However, the similarities end there. Otters are large and spend much of their time in water. They are probably more abundant than people think, but they are very elusive creatures. Finding signs of otters is easier than seeing the real thing. Their web-footed tracks are distinctive in soft mud, but the most important otter signs are spraints (droppings).

Evidence of Otters

Otter droppings are smeared onto rocks and logs as scent markers, often in small groups, with some fresher than others. They are small in proportion to the otter itself, only about 2 to 3 inches (6 to 8 cm) long and rather slender. They look tarry and black, almost like a patch of thick oil. Closer inspection reveals characteristic fragments of prey—fish bones, scales, and bits of crayfish or crabs, for example. Unlike the droppings of most mustelids, they do not smell unpleasant to humans.

Otters are riparian species, meaning that they frequent river banks, lake edges, and other waterside habitats. In a few places, Ireland and western Scotland, for example, they may live along the coast, feeding on rockpool fish and crabs. Wherever they live, otters need a secure place close to water in which to shelter during the day. A single animal may use more than 20 different lairs, often among tree roots or above ground. Sometimes they make a soft couch from grass and twigs, deep in a thicket.

An otter can travel over 6 miles (10 km) in a night and sometimes uses 50 miles (80 km) of river in a year. Coastal otters usually have much smaller territories, only a mile or so long. That is

⊕ *A European otter possesses short, dense underfur and long guard hairs, which are essential for keeping the animal well insulated in water.*

perhaps because food is more abundant, since rockpool fish are easier to catch than the bigger fish found in rivers. Large rivers are not necessarily best for otters and they often hunt in streams and tributaries. There is more food here, and it is easier to catch fish in pools and shallow streams than in larger bodies of water. The otter's ears are quite small, but hearing is still very acute. Sight is also good, and the sense of smell is likewise very important: Underwater, sight and touch are the main senses used.

On land otters can run at speeds equivalent to a fast walking pace, but in the water they can swim faster than humans. Otters are well adapted for life in water. They have webbed feet for swimming, and the long tail forms a rudder behind. The lithe body twists and turns to allow swift changes of direction and detailed exploration of underwater nooks and crannies.

Otter Conservation

Once a population of a scarce species becomes small and thinly dispersed, it is highly vulnerable to extinction. Boosting the population by releasing captive-bred animals may help save a species. That has been attempted in Britain and may be tried elsewhere. Beginning in 1983, captive-bred otters were released into river systems to fill gaps in the wild otter population. The animals soon bred. It is known that at least 25 otters were added to the local population in eastern England. The use of captive-bred animals has been criticized because they have been produced by a limited number of animals and might be inbred. However, all rare animals risk inbreeding—even in the wild. Restocking with unrelated animals may actually help reduce the problem. Further support can be given to otters by providing suitable lying-up sites in the form of planted thickets or mounds of earth and logs at the water's edge.

The fur is very thick, allowing the otter to remain warm and dry even in freezing-cold water. However, as it dives, increasing water pressure squeezes air out of the fur, leaving a characteristic trail of bubbles rising to the surface. The insulating effect of the fur is therefore reduced, causing loss of body heat. That is one reason why otters normally only dive in shallow water where the water pressure is less. The air in the fur also creates buoyancy, making it hard work to stay underwater, so the otters soon get out of breath. Dives are therefore short, and otters rarely stay submerged for more than about 30 to 40 seconds. They also spend less than 20 to 30 minutes in the water before coming ashore to get warm. They shake their fur dry, sometimes running around with an arched body or rolling in the grass.

Versatile Hunters

Otters are predators and feed on a wide variety of prey caught in the water, including fish weighing several pounds, frogs, and crustaceans. However, they also catch land animals such as rabbits and the occasional bird. They are very flexible in their hunting behavior, being able to adjust their technique to cope with whatever opportunities arise. They will nuzzle submerged stones to catch crayfish hiding underneath, grope in muddy water to feel for fish among tree roots, or grab a sleeping bird on its nest. Most of their diet consists of fish seized in the teeth. Shallow pools are best, because the fish cannot easily get away, and the otter can breathe every few seconds. Many dives are unsuccessful, but in shallow rockpools the animals might find food every once in three dives. Otters need the equivalent of about three 1-pound (0.5-kg) fish per day to satisfy their hunger.

Otters normally live alone or in a family group. They occasionally emit a loud whistle and also make a sharp bark, but otherwise they are not particularly vocal animals. Captive otters play a lot, but play seems to be relatively rare behavior in the wild and usually involves only

young animals. Adults cannot spare much energy for play—the effort and time are better spent searching for food. Adults do not often meet in the wild; and when they do, there may be a serious fight, especially between rival males. Fights involve squealing and chasing and sometimes biting, until one of the animals gives up and runs away. If a male and female meet, they may indulge in vigorous romping on land and in the water. Mating takes up to half an hour and happens either on land or while swimming. Afterward, the two animals separate

⊕ The European otter's lithe, elongated body and webbed feet are built for vigorous swimming. The long tail forms an effective rudder and allows for deft maneuvers when searching for food.

Otter cubs suckle frequently and make little chirruping noises. They grow slowly, taking five weeks or more to reach 2 pounds (0.9 kg) in weight—the size at which the eyes begin to open. Cubs take solid food from about seven weeks of age, but it will be another three weeks before they venture outside the den to play. Otters are three months old before they first start to swim, and the mother may still be catching over three-quarters of the food for cubs nearly eight months old. The cubs finally leave home when they are about a year old. New-found independence is a very tricky time, and many young otters die as they search for a territory of their own. Few otters survive more than five years, and probably only one in 100 reaches 10 years of age.

Chemical Poisoning

The main threats to European otters are food shortages and accidents, especially getting run over on the roads. Some otters get caught in fish traps and drown. Others fall victim to insecticides used to protect crops. Toxins build up in the animals' bodies, killing them or leaving them infertile.

Across Europe the effects of industrial pollution and acid rain are affecting the food supplies of fish on which the otters depend. Otters are becoming scarce or even extinct over wide areas as a result. However, strict pollution controls have allowed otters to survive in parts of western Europe from which they may slowly recolonize suitable habitat once the threats have been removed. Repopulation is already happening in Britain, which now probably has more otters with a healthier future than almost any other country in western Europe.

and go about their solitary lives. The male does not help raise the family—all the support needed by the cubs is provided by their mother.

Otters can breed at any time of the year where the climate is not too severe and food is always available. Although females can have a litter every year, nearly half of them probably only raise a family in alternate years. Gestation lasts just over two months, and the cubs are born in a special den, well above the level of rising flood waters. There are usually two or three cubs, but there may be up to five.

⤓ Fresh out of the water, the long guard hairs in an otter's pelt tend to stick together creating a spiky appearance.

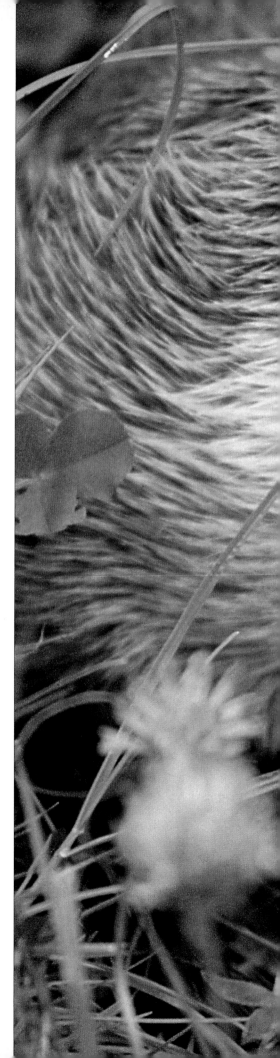

Disappearing Otters

The first survey of otter distribution in Britain was carried out in the mid-1950s. The animals were found to be widespread and fairly common, despite decades of hunting for sport. Otters were even reported on the fringes of London. However, by the 1960s some surveys were reporting reduced success. By the late 1970s fewer than 6 percent of sites inspected over large parts of southern and central England still had signs of otters. Otters were given full legal protection from 1978, but numbers continued to fall. Meanwhile, the Dutch otter population increased tenfold following legal protection. However, it is now extinct, proving that protective legislation alone is not the answer. Research has identified causes of decline that are potentially more dangerous to otters than hunting. The otter's demise coincided with the spread of the introduced American mink and a massive increase in fishing and boating.

Habitat destruction is another threat, especially the clearance of riversides, since tree roots provide otters with both lairs and sheltered backwaters in which to catch fish. However, the main problem for the otter was the introduction of new agricultural pesticides in the 1960s. Tiny amounts washed into ditches and streams, and were taken up by plankton. The plankton was eaten by fish, which were in turn consumed by otters.

Long-lived species like otters are especially vulnerable, since adults steadily accumulate the toxic chemicals, but stay alive, giving no sign that anything is wrong. However, breeding success is reduced long before poisoning is fatal. If the adults cannot breed, the population collapses when the older animals die, since there are too few offspring to keep it going.

Many dangerous agricultural chemicals have now been phased out, but another danger has emerged—this time from industrial sources. New chemicals called PCBs (polychlorinated biphenyls) are contaminating fish through pollution from factories and waste effluent, and are damaging at minute concentrations. Heavy metal pollutants (notably lead, mercury, and cadmium) also contaminate fish, especially eels, thereby damaging the health of predators like the otter. Pollution from acid rain creates yet more problems because it reduces the amount of insects and other food for fish, which in turn results in fewer otters. It may account for the disappearance of otters in parts of Central Europe.

European otters are scarce or declining in most areas, mainly as a result of habitat destruction and pollution. In some parts of Europe the species is now extinct.

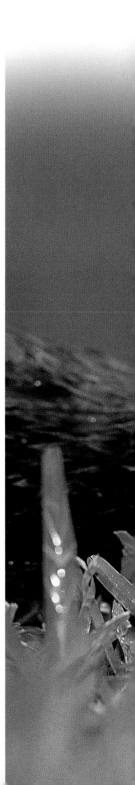

North American River Otter

Lontra canadensis

North American river otters are playful, intelligent animals that were once common throughout most of the United States and Canada. Many rivers are now too polluted or urbanized to support them.

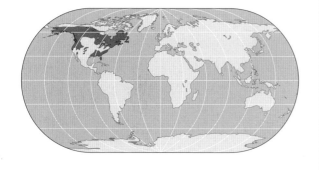

Common name North American river otter (northern river otter)

Scientific name *Lontra canadensis*

Family	Mustelidae
Order	Carnivora
Size	Length head/body: 26–42 in (66–107 cm); tail length: 12–20 in (32–46 cm); height at shoulder: 10–12 in (25–30 cm). Male larger than female
Weight	11–31 lb (5–14 kg)
Key features	Long, cylindrical body and short, stocky legs; long, pointed tail; small, blunt head with small ears and eyes; fur light to dark brown
Habits	Lively and playful: lives alone or in small groups; semiaquatic; active at any time of day
Breeding	Litters of 1–6 (usually 2 or 3) cubs born from November–May after gestation period of approximately 50 days (including delayed implantation). Weaned at 5–6 months; sexually mature at 2 or 3 years. May live to 21 years in captivity, 14 in the wild
Voice	Shrill chirps, soft "chuckles," grunts, coughs, and growls; loud screams when frightened
Diet	Mostly fish; also crayfish, frogs, crabs, birds' eggs, and small mammals
Habitat	Coastal and freshwater: rivers, streams, lakes, reservoirs, marshes, swamps, and estuaries
Distribution	Canada and mainly northwestern, southeastern, and Great Lakes states of U.S.
Status	Population: probably low thousands; CITES II. Common in some areas of U.S. and Canada, but extinct or rare in others

NORTH AMERICAN RIVER OTTERS used to be found in all the major waterways of the United States and Canada until at least the 18th century. Along with the beaver and timber wolf, otters were the most widely distributed wild mammals in the United States. They favor coastal areas, estuaries, rivers, lakes, and streams—in fact, any healthy water systems that can provide them with plenty of fish. Yet they are shy animals and do not like disturbance. When waterways are developed for housing, industry, or recreation, the otters usually leave. Even away from cities and towns agriculture poses a threat to otter habitats by removing tree and scrub cover and polluting water with pesticides. Because otters are at the top of the food chain, they are sensitive to any pollutants. Another threat to otter survival is the fur trade. About 20,000 to 30,000 animals are harvested every year. Such large numbers may actually be sustainable as long as the otters' habitat is healthy. Sadly, this is frequently not the case, and pollution, disturbance, and loss of habitat have brought about the extinction of otters in many areas.

Favorite Games

Otters are intelligent, quick, curious, and exuberant creatures. They are famous for their playful nature and will make a game of any activity. The young and even adults will play games of tag, tumbling, and wrestling. A favorite pastime is sliding down mud or snow banks into the water, tobogganing on their belly with their front legs folded back. Small objects such as shells, stones, or sticks are used as toys and for games of hide and seek. In captivity otters have been shown to have good memories and can be trained to perform tricks such as retrieving objects.

American river otters are well adapted to their aquatic life. They have a long, streamlined body and feet with webbed toes. The fur is dense and oily, with long, glossy guard hairs. Long, sensitive whiskers help the otter locate prey in murky water, and the small eyes are set high on the head and close to the nose, so the otter can look around above water while keeping most of its body submerged.

Otters are very graceful in the water. They swim by twisting their hind quarters and tail from side to side. They have a top speed of 6 to 7 miles per hour (10 to 11

km/h) and can dive to at least 60 feet (18 m) deep. They can stay submerged for over four minutes, but most dives are shallow and brief.

Waterway Travelers

Otters can have very large home ranges and may use many miles of waterway. Males generally travel farther than females. The length of a home range can vary from 5 to 50 miles (8 to 80 km), with the size depending on habitat quality. An otter living in an area with plenty of food, for example, will not have to travel as far as one that lives where prey is scarce. Territories of individual animals may overlap, and the home range of a male usually crosses that of one or more females.

Within their territories American river otters have many resting sites and dens. Rather than digging their own dens, they usually use holes

⊕ North American river otters are not as widespread as they once were and are now mostly confined to Canada and the northwestern, southeastern, and Great Lakes states of the United States.

made by other animals, such as beavers. They otherwise use natural shelters such as hollow tree trunks, driftwood piles, or even abandoned boathouses. Nursing dens have an underwater entrance with a tunnel leading to a nesting chamber lined with leaves, grasses, mosses, and hair to provide a soft bed for the young.

Scent Marking

Otters mark their territory using scent. Like other members of the weasel family, an otter has scent glands near its anus that produce a strong-smelling musk, which the animal wipes onto scent posts throughout its territory. They may be tree stumps, prominent stones, or logs, usually well above the water line so that scent marks do not get washed off by rising water levels after rain. As well as depositing musk, otters leave spraints (feces), which provide messages for the inquisitive noses of otters who visit later. Scent posts are usually in obvious places on the otter's route, including dens, rolling places, slides, runways, and haul-outs. Otters will also scratch up mounds of soil and debris or twist tufts of grass together, marking them with scent deposits or spraint. As well as defining boundaries, scent marking also signals when the otter last passed through, its sex, and probably its age, helping avoid potential conflict with other otters.

Although generally solitary, otters will spend time in a small group, which can be made up of a mother and her pups, a male and

⊕ A river otter with young by a stream in Montana. The young are born blind and helpless, but fully furred. They are introduced to water at about seven weeks, but are often reluctant swimmers and have to be dragged there.

female together, or even a group of bachelor males. Groups are temporary, have no apparent leader, and do not cooperate in hunting or share what is caught.

Most American river otters start to breed when they are two years old. Receptive females advertise their condition by markings at scent stations, and the powerful smell may attract two or three males. Although American river otters do not form strong pair bonds, once a male has mated, he may drive away other males who come near the female while she is receptive. He will then leave her and takes no part in rearing the offspring. However, sometimes fathers have been known to rejoin the family group when the young are about six months old. The young are born between November and May, but usually in March or April. The pups are born blind and helpless, but fully furred, and look like miniature versions of the adults.

Reluctant Swimmers

Otter milk is very rich, and the young grow quickly on it. They open their eyes at about four weeks and begin playing with each other and their mother. The mother introduces the pups to water by the time they are seven weeks old: They are often reluctant swimmers and may need to be dragged into the water. A mother will spend a lot of time teaching her pups, catching small fish and releasing them again so the young otters can develop their hunting skills. By nine or 10 weeks of age they start to eat solid food, although they will not be fully weaned until they are at least three months old. They are not fully independent for a further six months, but sometimes members of a family will stay together for a year or two.

Otters eat lots of fish, along with smaller amounts of other prey. They consume up to 2 pounds (1 kg) of food in a single meal. They have a rapid metabolism, so they need to eat frequently. When hunting, they spend a lot of time diving and chasing fish or digging in mud and stones at the bottom of ponds and streams for smaller prey. Crayfish are an important part of the diet, as are crabs along the seashore. Otters catch prey in the mouth, not the paws. Small food items are eaten in the water, while larger ones are taken ashore.

Otters tend to catch large or slow-moving fish. During salmon spawning times otters feast on the hordes of fish concentrated into small streams or shallow pools with nowhere to escape—exhausted "spawned-out" salmon are easy to catch. For most of the year, however, otters depend on other types of fish. Although fast-swimming species such as trout and pike are common in rivers and lakes, otters usually

Signs of Otter Activity

Otters are shy and elusive; few people are lucky enough to see them. However, it is relatively easy to find clues to their activity. When they come out of the water, they roll on the bank to dry themselves, leaving large areas of flattened vegetation. In soft mud their footprints show the distinctive marks of the webs between their toes. Spraints may also be visible—sometimes on twisted tufts of grass or piles of dirt and vegetation.

go for easier prey. They do not deserve the bad name given by anglers: Otters eat some sport fish, but are more likely to eat other species that actually compete with sport fish for food.

Otters will sometimes eat waterfowl, such as coots and ducks, and raid their nests for eggs. They may take dead or injured birds, particularly in the shooting season, but will also actively hunt and kill healthy birds. They stalk them by swimming underwater and grabbing the birds from below. Otters are also among the few predators that kill snapping turtles. Occasionally, otters will stalk birds and mammals on land. There have been reports of American river otters chasing and catching small mammals up to the size of snowshoe hares. They will also eat berries, such as rosehips and blueberries, but that is unusual.

⊕ An otter feeds on a trout caught in a river. Generally, river otters will take large or slow-moving fish rather than fast-swimming species, such as trout. During salmon spawning times otters will feast on exhausted fish resting in shallow pools.

Giant River Otter

Pteronura brasiliensis

The giant river otters of South America have been severely reduced in numbers as a result of hunting for their fur. They also suffer from habitat damage, but fortunately, small populations survive in protected areas.

GIANT RIVER OTTERS LIVE IN family groups of six to eight animals, although sometimes there can be as many as 20 individuals living together. Groups usually consist of a mated pair, along with their young born that year and often a few animals from the previous year as well. Giant otters are the most sociable of all the world's otter species. They stay close together, often calling loudly to each other or indulging in play. The adult male and female often share the same den, a habit that is not seen in the more familiar river otters of the Northern Hemisphere. Giant otters are also believed to help each other by driving shoals of fish into shallow water where they can be caught more easily. They usually feed on slow-moving species, such as catfish, which are easy to catch. Some such fish can be over 2 feet (60 cm) long.

Coveted Fur

The giant river otter is the largest of the freshwater otter species, and has a distinctive flattened tail. As with other types of otter, the fur is dense and helps protect the animal from getting cold when in the water. However, the giant otter's fur is very distinctive, being short and glossy, like velvet. It became particularly sought after in the 1960s when wearing furs was very fashionable. Native hunters could earn more money by selling a single giant otter skin than they would get in their pay packets for working hard as laborers for two or three months. The same skin would be worth five

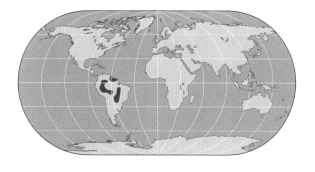

Common name
Giant river otter

Scientific name *Pteronura brasiliensis*

Family   Mustelidae

Order   Carnivora

Size   Length head/body: 34–55 in (86–140 cm); tail length: 13–39 in (33–100 cm); height at shoulder: 16 in (40 cm)

Weight Male 57–75 lb (26–34 kg); female 48–57 lb (22–26 kg)

Key features Large otter with short, glossy brown fur that looks black when wet; often white or creamy nose and throat; webbed feet; tail tapers and is flattened with a flange along each edge

Habits   Lives in family groups, mostly in the water

Breeding   Up to 5 young born in a single litter each year after gestation period of 65–70 days. Weaned at 3–4 months; sexually mature at 2 years. May live over 14 years in captivity, possibly similar in the wild

Voice   Loud yelps, barks, and whistles; very vocal

Diet   Mainly fish, but also freshwater crabs and occasional mammals

Habitat   Slow-moving rivers, creeks, and swamps, especially within forested areas

Distribution Once over much of tropical South America south to Argentina; now rare and patchy

Status   Population: perhaps fewer than 2,000 left in the wild; IUCN Endangered; CITES I

    SEE ALSO Otter, European **1**:58; Otter, North American River **1**:64; Otter, Sea **1**:72

Giant otters are mainly active during the daytime and so expose themselves to many dangers, particularly from humans with spears or guns. Giant otters are also very vocal, frequently calling to each other using a wide range of squeals, barks, and whistles. Their noise draws attention to them and makes it easier for hunters to locate and kill whole family groups. Another fatal characteristic is that giant otters are very curious animals: They often swim around with their heads held high out of the water to keep an eye on their surroundings—a habit that makes them easy to shoot. They will often swim toward intruders and potentially dangerous situations to investigate more closely—again making it easier to shoot them and to kill others of the group that stay around to see what has happened.

A Host of Threats

As huge areas of the South American forests were opened up for logging, new roads and tracks made it much easier to reach places that had otherwise been remote retreats for the giant otter. Gold mining has been a problem, too: Large amounts of cyanide and other poisonous pollutants have been released into the rivers where the otters live. Dredging for gold also makes rivers very muddy, which severely reduces the fish populations needed by the otters. People fish the rivers, too, removing still more of the otter's food supply.

It is little wonder that giant otter populations collapsed, and soon the species seemed to be heading for early extinction. Trade was banned in 1970, but there was considerable black market activity, and skins were smuggled through countries where law enforcement was slack. Nowadays otter skins are not fashionable, so the market no longer richly rewards hunters for killing the animals. Fortunately, giant otters are still fairly numerous in the Pantanal (bordering Brazil and Paraguay) and in parts of Peru. Some of the best habitats are relatively secure in national parks, and today the giant river otter enjoys full legal protection.

⊕ *The giant river otter of South America is the most sociable of all the otter species—a characteristic that has sadly helped decimate populations. Nowadays it is a rare sight.*

times as much in the fur trade after processing. Financial rewards provided a major incentive for hunters to kill otters, and in the 1950s over a thousand giant otter skins were exported each year from Peru alone. Since otters reproduce slowly, with only a single litter each year, breeding rates were not enough to keep up with such high levels of loss.

Common name Short-clawed otter

Scientific name *Amblonyx (Aonyx) cinereus*

Family	Mustelidae
Order	Carnivora
Size	Length head/body: 16–25 in (41–64 cm); tail length: 10–14 in (25–35 cm); height at shoulder: 8 in (20 cm)

Weight 2–11 lb (1–5 kg)

Key features Slender animal with short legs; upperparts dark or grayish-brown; chin, throat, cheeks, and sides of neck cream colored; fingers and toes only partially webbed; claws short

Habits Active by day; usually seen in groups; male and female appear to pair permanently; feeds in shallow water

Breeding One or 2 litters per year of 1–6 pups born after gestation period of 60–64 days. Weaned at about 80 days; sexually mature at 2–3 years. May live for 16 years in captivity, probably fewer in the wild

Voice Over a dozen different calls, including "wiuk" as a contact call

Diet Crabs, crayfish, mollusks, frogs, and small fish

Habitat Habitats where there is permanent water and some tree cover, including the coast, rivers, streams, ponds, lakes, and mangrove swamps

Distribution Northwestern India to southeastern China and Malay Peninsula; southern India; Sumatra, Java, Borneo, and Riau Archipelago (Indonesia); Palawan (Philippines)

Status Population: probably low thousands; IUCN Lower Risk: near threatened; CITES II. Relatively scarce and at risk in many places

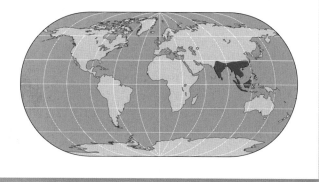

Short-Clawed Otter

Amblonyx cinereus

Short-clawed otters have unusual, handlike paws with almost nonexistent claws. The otters use their sensitive fingers to search in mud and under stones for food such as crabs.

THE ASIAN SHORT-CLAWED OTTER is the smallest of the world's otter species. As its name suggests, it has only very tiny claws. In adults they are tiny, blunt spikes that do not project beyond the tips of the fingers and toes. The feet are only partially webbed, up to the first finger and toe joints, which means that the otter cannot swim as powerfully as species that have fully webbed feet. Their paws are unusual among nonprimates in that they are handlike with nimble fingers and can be used for delicate manipulation of food. Short-clawed otters have an excellent sense of touch and coordination—they have even been seen juggling pebbles between their toes.

Nimble Fingers

Short-clawed otters use their sensitive and dexterous forepaws to find prey. They dig around in the mud or under stones in shallow rivers and pools, feeling for prey with their fingers. Because they tend to hunt in shallow water for crabs, mollusks, and other slow-moving food, they do not need to be such powerful swimmers as their fish-eating relatives. Their cheek teeth are enlarged and broadened for crushing crab and mollusk shells.

Short-clawed otters live in loose family groups of about 12 animals. Adults form long-lasting pair bonds in which the female is the dominant partner. Both parents help rear their offspring. Most pups stay with their parents even when they are grown up. The family forms the core of a small social group. Animals within a group are vocal, constantly communicating with each other using a wide variety of calls.

 SEE ALSO Otter, North American River **1**:64; Otter, Giant River **1**:68; Meerkat **1**:100

Fun and Games

Young short-clawed otters are social and playful creatures. They tumble, play chase and tug-of-war, slide down muddy hills, and are generally boisterous. When otters are not entertaining themselves, they bask on rocks, hunt for food, or go for a leisurely paddle. Unlike many other otters, they spend more time on land than in water, preferring shallows to deep water.

Short-clawed otters tend not to dig their own dens, since they lack strong claws. Instead, they usually make use of the abandoned dens of other animals or shelter in dense vegetation. In areas where there is little disturbance, short-clawed otters are active during the day. In the rice paddies of Malaysia, where there are often many people around, they are largely nocturnal. Short-clawed otters are sociable and easily trained. In Southeast Asia fishermen train otters to help them at work by driving shoals of fish into their nets. The otters are put on a harness and allowed to keep any fish they catch.

Short-clawed otters often feed in flooded rice paddies. They can become unpopular with farmers because they sometimes uproot young rice plants while probing in the mud for food. However, they eat huge numbers of crabs, which are a pest in rice fields, so it is likely they do more good than harm.

Short-clawed otters are officially classed as at a lower risk of extinction than some other otter species. However, in some parts of their range, such as in parts of Malaysia, deforestation is a serious problem because it opens up river valleys for development. Development means disturbance and often less food. Increasing use of pesticides and other pollutants also harms the otters, particularly since many of their prey species are very sensitive to pollution. Other threats include entanglement in fishing nets and fur trapping.

Asian short-clawed otters are part of a worldwide captive-breeding program that aims to protect the species from extinction. The program is focusing on the best ways of keeping and breeding them so no more need be taken from the wild.

⊕ *Short-clawed otters are very sociable and live in loose family groups numbering up to about 12. The young enjoy playing games, such as chase and tug-of-war.*

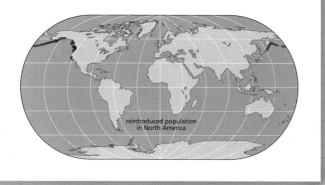

Common name Sea otter

Scientific name *Enhydra lutris*

Family	Mustelidae
Order	Carnivora
Size	Length head/body: 29.5–35 in (75–90 cm); tail length: 11–12.5 in (28–32 cm); height at shoulder: 8–10 in (20–25 cm)
	Weight 30–85 lb (14–38 kg)
Key features	Dark-brown otter with blunt-looking head that turns pale cream with age; feet completely webbed; hind feet form flippers
Habits	Floats on back in kelp beds and calm waters; dives to feed from seabed
Breeding	One pup born each year in early summer after gestation period of 4 months (including up to 8 months delayed implantation). Weaned at 5 months; females sexually mature at 3 years; males at 5-6 years, but do not breed successfully until at least 7 years. May live for over 20 years in captivity, similar in the wild
Voice	Normally silent
Diet	Crabs, shellfish, sea urchins, fish, and other marine animals
Habitat	Kelp beds and rocky seashores
Distribution	Formerly along coasts across eastern and northern Pacific from California to Kamchatka and northern Japan; exterminated over most of its range, now reintroduced to coasts of California, Alaska, Oregon, and Washington
Status	Population: about 150,000 and growing; IUCN Endangered; CITES II. Given full legal protection in 1911 and probably now secure

reintroduced population
in North America

Sea Otter

Enhydra lutris

The sea otter was once widespread along the coasts of the North Pacific, but hunting for skins brought the species to the brink of extinction. It has now substantially recovered, thanks to strict international protection and some successful reintroductions.

TODAY SEA OTTERS ARE EASILY observed, especially along the California coast, and their playful antics make them a popular species to watch. They spend most of their time floating quietly on their back at the water's surface, grooming their fur and rolling over and over in the waves. They also spend long periods dozing on their backs—often anchored by a strand of kelp draped across their chest. Periodically, they feed by making short dives of about a minute to the seabed to look for crabs, sea urchins, and mollusks. They cannot dive deeply, so they have to stay in relatively shallow waters. They also cannot last long without food and are unable to make long journeys out to sea if it entails crossing large areas of deep water. However, they do sometimes undertake long journeys along the coast, sticking close to shore where they can continue to feed along the way. Generally, sea otters are solitary animals, and males are territorial, probably to avoid competing for limited food resources.

Unwitting Conservationists

Sea otters are intelligent animals and have learned to bite open old drink cans that have sunk to the bottom of the ocean and now provide a lair in which a small octopus may hide. They also eat large numbers of sea urchins, helping control their numbers. Keeping numbers down is important because the urchins eat growing kelp. If there are too many urchins, the kelp beds are unable to flourish and do not protect the coast from the full force of the Pacific tides. Beach erosion and flooding may result. Hence sea otters are very important ecologically for maintaining a healthy coastline.

⊕ The sea otter possesses the densest coat of any mammal to help keep it warm in the chilly seas of the North Pacific. There are estimated to be over half a million hairs per square inch of fur.

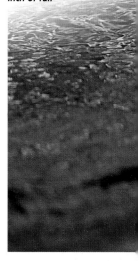

Densest Fur on Earth

Sea otters are probably the smallest warm-blooded animals that spend all their time in the water. The coastal seas of the North Pacific are very cold: Even far south off California the sea is cool and will chill a mammal's body quite quickly. The sea otter therefore needs very effective insulation to prevent loss of body heat. Its protection is provided by a thick coat of the densest fur possessed by any mammal. There are estimated to be more than half a million hairs per square inch on the sea otter's body—twice as many as found on the larger fur seals. The fur has long, shiny guard hairs that help keep the water at bay and prevent the underfur from becoming matted and losing its insulation value. Below the guard hairs is a dense mass of extremely fine underfur that traps a layer of air against the skin and acts as insulation to prevent heat loss.

The sea otter is totally dependent on its fabulous fur to enable it to live in the cold seas without becoming chilled. It therefore spends much of its time grooming and caring for its precious coat. That is also why the animal cannot dive deeply, since the increased water

⊕ *Sea otters make dives to the seabed to look for prey such as crabs, sea urchins, and mollusks. However, they easily get out of breath, so cannot dive deeply, and must stay in shallower waters along the coast.*

pressure at depth squeezes the vital air from the fur, causing it to lose its insulating properties. The trapped air also makes the otter rather buoyant, so it has to expend more energy swimming down into the water than would be needed by a small seal or whale. It soon gets out of breath, which prevents it from staying underwater long enough to reach greater depths. The otter's fur is not just valuable to the animal: For over 200 years it was also one of the world's most prized furs for human use, making warm coats for winter wear. A sea otter's skin could be sold for the equivalent of an entire year's wages for a seaman, so there was plenty of incentive to hunt the otters. Hunting sea otters and fur seals was one of the main reasons for the early exploration of the North Pacific. During the 18th century Russian navigators expanded their trade in skins and colonized Alaska and what is now British Columbia, as well as the Aleutian Islands. Later the British and Americans joined in.

Skin Trade

Over three-quarters of a million sea otters were killed between 1750 and 1850, with 17,000 skins in a single shipment made in 1803. Pelts were bartered with the Chinese in exchange for fine porcelain, which could then be taken to Europe and sold for immense profits. Expeditions would stock up with axes and other useful tools made in Europe and North America, then sail back to the North Pacific and

⊕ *A sea otter feeds on shellfish while swimming on its back. Sea otters carry a flat stone to help them smash open hard shells. Prey is placed on the otter's stomach and crushed with the stone.*

trade the tools with local hunters for yet more sea otter pelts.

The otters were easily hunted from canoes and kayaks. An animal would be chased so it was forced to dive repeatedly until it was out of breath. When it was too exhausted to dive any more, the hunter speared it and dragged the body into the kayak, where it was skinned. The body was then thrown back into the sea, and the hunter paddled on to find the next otter. Since the otters only lived along the coast and did not seek safety by dispersing out at sea, they could be hunted systematically until every last one had been killed along hundreds of miles of coastline. Sea otters have few natural predators (killer whales, bears, and bald eagles occasionally kill them) and are not adapted to withstand heavy losses. They do not breed rapidly and produce only one youngster per year—often not even every year. Females do not breed until they are over three years old and sometimes can be over five years old before producing their first baby. Male sea otters take even longer to mature and may not have a breeding territory established until they are 10 years old.

Slow breeding meant that sea otter populations could not cope with heavy exploitation, and the animals soon disappeared over wide areas. By the early 20th century the sea otter had become exceedingly rare, having been reduced to perhaps fewer than a thousand animals in the whole North Pacific. It was on the brink of total extinction. Yet its range crossed several international borders so giving it legal protection in one country would not necessarily help: The animals might be killed illegally in one country, but then smuggled out to be sold somewhere else. What was needed was an international agreement to give the animal legal protection everywhere. However, that had never been done before for any marine animal. In 1911, in the first such international agreement, the Russians, Americans, and British (on behalf of Canada) agreed to total protection for the sea otter throughout the North Pacific.

Tool User

The sea otter is one of the few animals, apart from apes, that has learned to use tools. It often carries a flat stone tucked into its armpit and uses it to help smash open the hard shells of the crabs, mollusks, and sea urchins on which it feeds. The otter lies on its back, floating in calm water, with its prey lying on its chest. The animal uses its paws to lift the stone and hit the prey hard and repeatedly, crushing it against its chest until the juicy insides are exposed and can be eaten.

Repopulation Success

Slowly, sea otters have regained their numbers, and today there are about 150,000 of them, about half the number that probably existed 300 years ago. Gradually, they are spreading back to many parts of the coast where they have been extinct for more than a century. It was once thought that sea otters had been eradicated from the California coast, but a few were spotted in 1938, and numbers have lately increased to more than 2,000. Fishermen now say there are too many of them—complaining that the otters eat too many mollusks, crabs, and other valuable sea creatures. Population growth leveled out in the late 1970s, and a small decline may even have taken place since 1998, perhaps indicating that the habitat cannot sustain any more, and sea otters are back at their natural population size.

In an attempt to speed up the recolonization of the sea otter's former haunts, surplus animals have been transported to Washington State, Oregon, and Alaska to repopulate areas along those coasts. Overall the sea otter seems now to have a secure and expanding future in the North Pacific. However, there are new dangers, notably from oil spills near the coast. Detergents used to clean up oil spills are almost as dangerous. Another threat comes from TBT (tri butyl tin), a substance found in the special paint used to prevent barnacles and seaweeds growing on the hulls of boats. The substance also kills other forms of marine life, including some of the main foods of the sea otter. Nevertheless, the sea otter's comeback is one of the best examples of successful international cooperation to secure the conservation of a rare animal.

⊕ The sea otter's dark-brown coloration turns pale cream on the head with age, as with this adult. Sea otters may live for over 20 years and are now a fully protected species.

Common name American badger

Scientific name *Taxidea taxus*

Family	Mustelidae
Order	Carnivora
Size	Length head/body: 16.5–28 in (42–72 cm); tail length: 4–6 in (10–15 cm); height at shoulder: 8–10 in (20–25 cm)
Weight	Male 18–26.5 lb (8–12 kg); female 13–18 lb (6–8 kg)
Key features	Flattened body with short legs, long curved foreclaws, and shovel-like hind claws; gray to yellowish-brown fur with cream belly; sides of face white; dark patches behind ears and on cheeks; white stripe from forehead to nose
Habits	Forages at night; does not hibernate; solitary, except for breeding pairs and family groups
Breeding	Litters of 1–5 young born late March or early April after gestation period of 7 months (including 5.5 months delayed implantation). Weaned at 6 weeks; female sexually mature at 12 months, male at 14 months. May live for 26 years in captivity, 12–14 in the wild
Voice	Normally silent, but occasional yelps
Diet	Mainly burrowing mammals such as pocket gophers and ground squirrels; also birds, reptiles, insects, and occasionally some plants
Habitat	Treeless regions, prairies, meadows, and cold desert areas
Distribution	Parts of Canada, U.S., and Mexico
Status	Population: unknown, perhaps low thousands. Increasing, but still uncommon

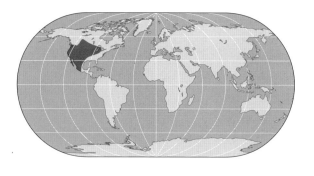

American Badger

Taxidea taxus

The American badger catches most of its food by digging. It can tunnel with amazing speed and will turn over vast amounts of soil in its nightly hunts.

AMERICAN BADGERS HAVE A BODY built for digging. With their powerful claws and partially webbed toes they can move through soil surprisingly quickly. There are stories of badgers digging through asphalt roads. The animals have a third eyelid (a nictating membrane) to protect their eyes from dust. Loose skin on their back and shoulders gives them mobility in tight tunnels.

Multipurpose Dens

Dens are the center of badger life. They are usually simple tunnels with one entrance. Soil excavated in making the den is piled up outside. When badgers are in the den, especially during cold weather, they will sometimes block the entrance with loose soil to help keep warm. The dens used by females to give birth and rear the family are more complex. The side tunnels branch off and rejoin the main thoroughfare, allowing the badgers to pass each other. There are additional side tunnels and chambers, sometimes containing grassy nesting material. Shallow pockets off the main tunnel are dug as latrines and covered in soil. Since they are so extensive, nursing dens have larger piles of soil outside than normal dens. Mounds often contain fur because they are dug in spring when the badger is molting.

American badgers are uniquely adapted for catching underground prey. They dig into burrows to catch pocket gophers, ground squirrels, and many smaller rodents. However, they will also take advantage of whatever other food is available and will eat many small creatures, including snakes, toads, frogs, birds, insects and their grubs, wasps, bees, and worms. In addition they will occasionally eat

⊕ An American badger emerges from its den. Its powerful shoulders and strong claws make it exceptionally proficient at digging.

plant material, too, particularly in the fall, when they take sunflower seeds, corn, and other grains. They also eat carrion and are known to store food in old dens.

Badgers sometimes develop close associations with coyotes, tolerating their presence and even playing with them. The coyotes follow badgers while they are hunting, catching rodents that the badger flushes from burrows. Coyotes help the badgers find new burrowing and hunting areas, sometimes appearing to encourage them with "chase me" play behavior, and sharing the proceeds of their joint hunting efforts.

Plowing the Land

Badgers are an important part of their habitat because they act as miniplows, literally shaping the land. Their digging loosens the soil and creates patches where different types of plants can grow, increasing the diversity of prairie species. Their holes are often used as ready-made dens by other mammals and as nesting sites by birds such as burrowing owls.

Badgers have few natural enemies, since they are such ferocious fighters. Once they are over a year old and past their vulnerable stage, humans are probably the greatest threat. Many badgers are run over or die in traps set for fur-bearing animals. Others are poisoned by bait put down to control wolves and coyotes. Badger hair has been used to make shaving brushes, but on the whole the animals are not hunted for their fur.

Tolerated

Farmers generally tolerate badgers because they eat large numbers of rodents and will also kill venomous snakes. However, badger burrows can damage crops and are sometimes hazardous to livestock and machinery.

Badgers are one of the few larger mammals that are actually increasing their range in the United States. Because they live in treeless habitats, they benefit from logging and other human activities that open up the land.

Common name European badger

Scientific name *Meles meles*

Family	Mustelidae
Order	Carnivora
Size	Length head/body: 27.5–31 in (70–80 cm); tail length: 5–7 in (12–19 cm); height at shoulder: 12 in (30 cm)

Weight 18–26 lb (8–12 kg)

Key features Dog-sized animal with short legs and long, coarse hair, grizzled gray on back and black on belly; face is white with prominent black stripes running backward through the eyes

Habits Nocturnal; occupies a clan territory; often inactive for long periods in winter, but does not hibernate

Breeding Usually 1–4 cubs born around February after gestation period of 10–12 months (including 8–10 months delayed implantation). Weaned at about 4 months; sexually mature at 2 years. May live to be 16 years in captivity, 10 in the wild

Voice Occasional yelps and loud whickering noises

Diet Almost anything edible found at ground level, including worms, small mammals, roots, fruit, acorns, and beetles

Habitat Woodlands, farmlands, even suburban areas where there is access to food; prefers well-drained soils on slopes for burrowing

Distribution Widespread in most of Europe from Britain and Spain eastward to China and Japan

Status Population: probably at least 1.5 million. Generally scarce, even extinct in some areas, but increasingly common in parts of Britain

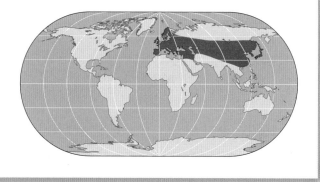

European Badger

Meles meles

Badgers are large, distinctive creatures that live in groups of closely related animals called clans. They are the most social members of the mustelid family.

BADGERS ARE GREAT DIGGERS and excavate an extensive burrow system called a sett. Normally there are about 10 entrances leading to a labyrinth of perhaps 100 yards (90 m) of tunnels and galleries. Main setts are the headquarters of the social group, which consists of closely related individuals collectively referred to as a clan. Often they have small "outlier" setts nearby that are not occupied continuously and are only visited for a few days or weeks during the late summer.

Badgers have special adaptations to help with digging, notably powerful limbs and big paws, each armed with long, curved claws on all five toes. The bones and muscles of the shoulders and forelimbs are specially modified to provide leverage for shifting stones and earth. Digging is done with the broad forepaws, and loose earth is scooped backward under the belly and kicked away with the hind feet.

Creature Comforts

Underground it is generally cool, and it may be damp as well. To make the sett more comfortable, badgers import large amounts of bedding in the form of dry grass, bracken, or other suitable material. They rake up the grass using their front paws, tuck a bundle between the forearms and chin, and shuffle backward to the sett. Badgers are scrupulously clean animals. They use a special toilet area outside the sett so their underground nests do not become fouled. Nevertheless, the bedding gets soggy after a few months, and badgers usually clean it out at the end of winter, leaving a large heap outside.

SEE ALSO Badger, American **1:**76; Badger, Honey **1:**82; Lion **2:**14

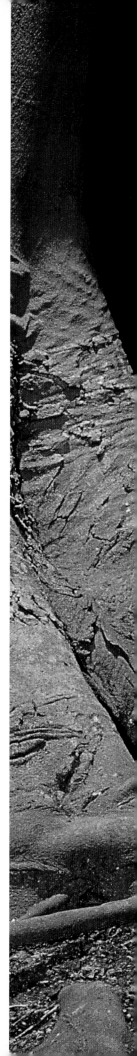

The badger's fur is coarse and sparse, but it protects the skin from damage and does not get clogged with dirt: A quick scratch with the long claws, and all the mess falls away. Badgers spend a lot of time scratching when they go above ground each evening, especially to get the soil out of their coat. However, the sparse wiry hairs do not provide much insulation, so instead of having a layer of fluffy underfur close to the skin to keep them warm, badgers accumulate large amounts of fat as an insulating layer under the skin. Fat is also useful as a food reserve that can be drawn on over winter. Badgers are not true hibernators, but they do remain inactive underground during long periods of inclement weather, relying on their fat reserves to tide them over until conditions improve.

Social and Solitary

Badgers live in groups, but they are not social to the same extent as lions, for example. They do not help each other raise young or hunt and travel in herds or packs. Each adult badger spends practically all of its active periods above ground alone. It hunts alone, travels alone, and feeds alone. Badger social behavior is therefore less developed than that of many monkeys, but more highly organized than in seals, which live in large groups once a year only for the purposes of breeding.

A special benefit of living in a group is that it is easier to defend territory. Instead of each

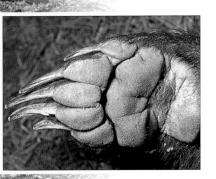

badger defending its own individual territory, a whole group of related animals (the clan) defends a communal patch of land, which may be over 250 acres (100 ha) in extent.

⊖ *With five sharp, curved claws on each paw (inset), European badgers are well adapted for a life of rooting for food and digging underground tunnels.*

79

Badger Mobility

Badgers amble around with a rolling flat-footed gait, like bears. They slow down to sniff and search carefully for food. When alarmed, a badger can sprint at 20 miles per hour (32 km/h), but not for long distances. It can also climb, using its claws and powerful forelimbs to grip rough stonework or the bark of logs. Sloping trees are often explored, and badger hairs may be found more than 10 feet (3 m) above the ground.

A cub forages for food in a British woodland.

Resident badgers tolerate each other, while intruders are chased off. The animals recognize each other by their scent. Smell is useful for a nocturnal animal because visual signals are hard to see in the dark, especially in the thick scrub and bushes often frequented by badgers. Scent also makes recognition possible at a distance, and scent marks and feces are left around the territory to warn off badger trespassers.

Many Paws Make Light Work

Living in a social group has other advantages. If badgers lived alone, each would have to dig its own burrow—hard work for an animal of such a size, since the tunnels have to measure about 12 inches (30 cm) in diameter. Even a small sett needs a ton or more of earth to be dug out. In a shared sett each badger can simply use the same passages and entrance as other animals and might never dig much at all. The whole sett can be handed down through the generations, providing all the advantages of a complex burrow system with little work to do except keep it clean and perhaps dig occasional extensions. As a result, more time and energy are left for feeding, breeding, and play.

Play is common among social animals. It helps bond the members of a social group and

enables them to recognize each other. Badgers also groom one another and may lick each other's fur—all part of the system for creating social bonds. Normally, a badger social group consists of about six animals, but sometimes there may be over 20. Each clan usually has a dominant male. He and the other males are more active in scent marking their communal territory than the females and consequently move around more within the group's area. Territorial activity is greatest in the early spring and is the time that most bite wounds are found, particularly among males.

Breeding is normally confined to the main sett, and only one family of cubs will be produced, with most of the females in the clan not breeding. In some carnivores, nonbreeding females often act as helpers and assist in bringing up the dominant female's family. But in the badger home only the mother suckles the young and takes them out to forage. Badgers do not seem to use helpers, and the nonbreeders contribute little to the welfare of the breeding group. Males sometimes play with the cubs, but do not help feed them. Most cubs born within the group are fathered by the males in that same group. However, some boars manage to sneak into neighboring social groups and mate successfully with females there. While most badgers stay with their clan all their life, some older males may go to live elsewhere, which helps prevent inbreeding. However, such individuals take a great risk. Newcomers often get savagely attacked by resident badgers and sustain serious bite wounds, which may get infected and lead to a lingering death.

Meat and Vegetable Diet

At dusk the badgers emerge from their sett, have a good scratch, and go off to feed. Badgers eat worms, small mammals, beetles, and frogs, and they will relish a nestful of baby rabbits or birds' eggs. But although they are members of the order Carnivora, badgers have a broad diet and eagerly dig up a wasps' nest or root out bluebell bulbs, wild arum corms, and even garden bulbs in the spring. Fruit such as blackberries, bilberries, and fallen apples are a favorite in the fall. Beech mast and acorns are also crunched up in large quantities.

The badger is well adapted for its varied diet. The molar teeth are broad and knobby for grinding up tough nuts and gritty worms, and the jaws have such a strong hinge that they cannot be dislocated. A willingness to eat vegetable material leads the badger into unpopular activities, such as raiding cereal crops. Besides eating the grain, they also roll in the ripening crop, making it difficult to harvest.

Badgers normally reach breeding age when they are two years old. They mate during the spring, but the development of the embryos is delayed for many weeks before normal pregnancy starts. The delay ensures that the cubs are born at the best time of year, usually in February. At first they have pink skin covered with a thin layer of silky white fur. The facial stripes are barely visible. The cubs spend about eight weeks underground and will not be fully weaned until they are about 16 weeks old. They grow quickly and can weigh as much as 20 pounds (9 kg) by the end of their first year.

⊛ As carriers of bovine tuberculosis, European badgers have come into conflict with farmers, particularly in Britain. To combat the disease, culls have taken place in Britain and Ireland, although their effectiveness is in doubt.

Common name Honey badger (ratel)

Scientific name *Mellivora capensis*

Family   Mustelidae

Order   Carnivora

Size   Length head/body: 24–30 in (60–77 cm); tail length: 8–12 in (20–30 cm); height at shoulder: 10–12 in (25–30 cm)

Weight 15.5–28.5 lb (7–13 kg)

Key features Solidly built animal with short tail and short, sturdy legs with extremely long, strong claws; fur usually grizzled gray on back, black to brown elsewhere; head small with short muzzle and small eyes

Habits   Nocturnal; excellent digger; usually solitary; extremely aggressive

Breeding One to 4 (usually 2) young born at any time of year after gestation period of 6 months. Weaning and sexual maturity unknown. May live up to 26 years in captivity, perhaps 10 in the wild

Voice   Harsh growls when angry

Diet   Mammals, reptiles, poisonous snakes, birds, insects, and worms; also carrion, eggs, fruit, and honey

Habitat   Anywhere with suitable sites for dens—forests, grassy plains, and rocky slopes

Distribution Africa and southwestern Asia

Status   Population: unknown, probably a few thousand. Widespread but declining

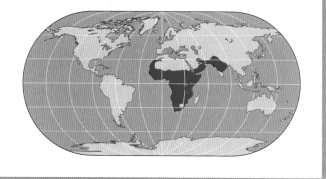

Honey Badger

Mellivora capensis

The honey badger is a natural aggressor. It will attack animals much larger than itself with remarkable ferocity. However, its fearlessness is not entirely unjustified, since the animal is very difficult to kill.

THE STRIKINGLY MARKED HONEY badger is a formidable animal. It is not particularly large and has a typically shambling, badgerlike appearance. However, it is without doubt one of the world's most relentlessly aggressive animals, always ready to pick a fight with almost any other living creature. Honey badgers have been known to attack horses, wild cattle, 11-foot (3.4-m) long pythons, deadly cobras, whole packs of domestic dogs, and any other animal they perceive as potential food or a possible threat. Attacks are often launched quite suddenly from a burrow or patch of dense vegetation. The honey badger will quite readily give up a perfectly secure location in order to attack an unsuspecting victim that appears to have done nothing to provoke it.

Fearless Attacker

The honey badger has large, strong teeth and long claws. While they certainly serve as effective weapons, they do not in themselves explain the extraordinary self-assurance with which the animal throws itself into combat. Its apparent fearlessness is not without justification, however, since the honey badger is extremely difficult to kill. It is protected all over with an immensely tough, rubbery skin that is thick enough not to be pierced by most teeth, including the needle-sharp fangs of venomous snakes. Its skin is also very loose fitting, which means that even if the honey badger is grabbed firmly by the neck, it can easily wriggle around and bite its attacker.

Despite its potential ferocity, the honey badger generally prefers to mind its own

business and is rarely seen in the open, even in areas where the species is still relatively common. It emerges from its den only at night and spends much of its time digging or sniffing around for small food items.

Sweet Tooth

As its common name suggests, the honey badger has a sweet tooth and is particularly fond of honey. It tracks down bees' nests—often by teaming up with an unlikely partner, a bird called the African honey guide. Unlike most small birds, which stay well away from a hungry honey badger, the honey guide actively seeks out the badger, attracting its attention with a special call. Honey guides like honey too, and they especially love the nutrient-rich wax honeycombs made by bees to store honey and grubs. However, the bird is not strong enough to break into a bees' nest on its own. Having discovered a hive, the honey guide calls for help. The honey badger follows the bird to the hive, breaks it open with its claws, and devours most of the honey. Its thick skin protects it from the stings of angry bees. Meanwhile, the honey guide gets its reward, feeding on the remaining broken honeycombs, which are now widely scattered and accessible owing to the badger's destruction of the nest. Other creatures also benefit from the honey badger's strength and foraging abilities. The black-backed jackal, for example, pounces on rodents and reptiles flushed out by the badger. The badger gains no advantage from association with the jackal.

The breeding biology of honey badgers is not well known. Animals are sometimes seen traveling in pairs, but usually they are solitary. The young are born in spring in the north of the species' range, but breeding appears to be less seasonal in much of Africa. Gestation lasts up to six months, and the young are cared for in a secure den lined with dry grass.

⊖ *Although honey badgers find most of their food on the ground, they are known to scale tall camelthorn acacias in search of raptor bird chicks.*

Common name
　　Striped skunk

Scientific name *Mephitis mephitis*

Family　Mustelidae

Order　Carnivora

Size　Length head/body: 12.5–18 in (32–45 cm); tail length: 7–10 in (17–25 cm); height at shoulder: 4 in (10 cm). Male larger, but female has longer tail

Weight 3–13 lb (1.5–6 kg)

Key features Cat-sized animal, with small head tapering to a bulbous nose; black coat with forked white stripes on back; white patch and stripe on head; long, bushy tail

Habits　Mainly active at night and at dusk and dawn; generally solitary; squirts foul-smelling liquid when threatened; may swim if necessary

Breeding　Three to 9 young born May–June after gestation period of 62–66 days (including delayed implantation). Weaned at 6–8 weeks; sexually mature at 1 year. May live 8–10 years in captivity, fewer than 3 in the wild

Voice　Low growls, grunts, and snarls; also churring and short squeals; occasional screech or hiss

Diet　Mainly insects; also small rodents, rabbits, birds, eggs, carrion, fruit, vegetables, and garbage

Habitat　Forest or field edges, patches of brush, rocky outcrops, and wooded ravines; town gardens

Distribution Southern Canada, U.S., and northern Mexico

Status　Population: abundant

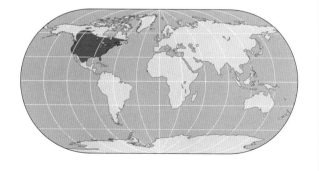

Striped Skunk

Mephitis mephitis

Skunks are one of the few mammals to use chemical defense. When threatened, they squirt a repulsive-smelling liquid at their attacker.

THE STRIPED SKUNK IS THE MOST common of the 10 species of skunk. All skunks live in North, Central, and southern America and do not occur anywhere else in the world. Skunks are sufficiently different from other mammals that they are frequently classified in a family of their own: the Mephitidae.

The striking black-and-white markings of striped skunks serve the same purpose as the stripes on a wasp—they are a warning signal. After a first unpleasant encounter any animal that sees another skunk will remember that the dramatic coloring is associated with a repugnant smell and will probably make a hasty retreat. The markings are variable, but usually consist of a predominantly dark body with a white blaze on the nose, a white hood, and white stripes that extend from the hood to the tail. The tail may be tipped with white, and there are often white spots on the legs and around the ears. The stripes on the back vary in length and width, so that an animal may appear almost entirely black or white or many variations in between. There is no difference in patterning between the sexes, and the markings do not change with the seasons.

Foul-Smelling Spray

A well-known fact about skunks is that they stink. Even their Latin name *Mephitis* means bad smell. The smell is their one effective defense mechanism, since skunks are not fast runners, vicious fighters, or clever at hiding. When a skunk is threatened, it will first give a warning display by raising its tail and repeatedly stamping its forefeet on the ground. If the warning is not heeded, the animal curves its body into a "C" shape so that it can point its

⊖ *A striped skunk rests on a log in a field of flowers. The white forked stripe that runs from its head to its haunches distinguishes it from other species.*

anus at the target while keeping a close eye on its adversary. The skunk then squirts a yellowish foul-smelling spray from muscular pouches on either side of the anus at the base of the tail.

The spray ("musk") comes through a nipple that can be angled to improve the skunk's aim. It can hit a target at a distance of up to 6.5 feet (2 m). Skunks are able to spray several times in quick succession, and the spray can either be a fine vapor or a more directed shower of droplets. The animals avoid spraying themselves and do not scatter the scent with their tail as many people believe.

The musk contains volatile sulfur compounds, like the smell from bad eggs, which is also sulfur based. Humans can smell it up to 1 mile (0.5 km) downwind; and if it gets into the eyes, it causes extreme pain and even temporary blindness. It takes up to 48 hours for the skunk to replace the musk. The posturing and displaying before the animal sprays is to give their attacker the chance to get away, thereby saving the valuable chemical.

Insects on the Menu

Striped skunks are omnivores. They are opportunistic feeders, eating almost anything that appears vaguely edible. About 70 percent of their diet is made up of insects, such as grasshoppers, crickets, beetles, bees, and wasps. One of their favorite foods is grubs, which they dig up from the soil. Striped skunks will also feed on spiders, snails, earthworms, clams, crayfish, frogs, salamanders, snakes, birds' eggs, small mammals, carrion, berries, nuts, roots, grains, and garbage.

Most food is located by sound or smell, since the skunks' distance vision is poor. In addition, the animals are too slow to chase fast-moving prey. Instead, they hunt like cats, lying in wait or stalking their victim. They catch beetles and grasshoppers by springing on them with their forepaws.

Urban Warriors

Urban areas provide everything that a skunk needs. Human mess means that there is always plenty of garbage to feed on, and where there is garbage, there are usually rats and mice as well. Skunks will also dig up lawns for grubs. They can live in burrows under buildings; and if there are several animals in residence, the smell can be overpowering.

Skunks are unwelcome in towns. Any human that gets too close is likely to be sprayed.

Females prepare maternity dens in March. The young are born in mid-May and are wrinkled, blind, and almost hairless. Even at birth the color patterns are visible as dark patches on the skin. Males do not help rear the kittens and may even attack or kill them, so females defend the maternity dens aggressively.

The kittens are fast-growing: After about three weeks they can assume the defensive posture and squirt scent. They are weaned at six to eight weeks and follow the mother on hunting trips when they are about two months old. When out with their mother, they keep close behind her in a single-file trail. By August they have reached adult size and are able to fend for themselves. They will be able to breed the following spring.

In summer skunks use dens above ground, selecting hollow logs or rock piles. In winter, although they do not hibernate, they rest for

They will use their long front claws to dig for grubs or to tear apart the nests of small mammals, such as mice, rats, moles, and ground squirrels. Striped skunks also break into beehives and will eat the inhabitants without appearing to be affected by the stings. They are known to consume the bee larvae and probably the honey, too. Skunks have a special trick for dealing with poisonous or hairy caterpillars. Before eating them, they roll the prey on the ground with their forepaws, an activity that successfully removes the irritant hairs or toxins in the skin. Striped skunks have also been seen breaking eggs by rolling them between the hind legs with their forepaws until the egg strikes a stone and cracks open.

A Skunk's Way of Life

Striped skunks are not social animals. They come together to breed in spring, but spend the rest of the year alone or in groups made up of mothers and their young. Females occupy a home range of 0.8 to 1.5 square miles (2 to 4 sq. km). Their territory will overlap that of many other females, but they tend to avoid contact with each other. The males travel much farther—about 8 square miles (20 sq. km)—and cover the home ranges of many females, as well as overlapping with other males. The males mate with many females living in their range.

 SEE ALSO Raccoon, Common 1:22

⟵ *Two young striped skunks take in the sounds and smells near their birthplace, a hollow log den.*

sometimes spend the winter in the same burrow as opossums, woodchucks, or cottontail rabbits, but occupy different chambers.

Death by Natural Causes

In captivity skunks may live for 10 years, but in the wild more than 90 percent never reach the age of three. Natural causes of death include starvation in harsh winters, predation, and disease. Skunks are preyed on by great horned owls and some other birds of prey—all of which have a poorly developed sense of smell. Mammalian predators will hunt them too, but only if on the verge of starvation. The smell is enough to deter all but the hungriest hunter.

A common cause of death in skunks is disease. Striped skunks are susceptible to many diseases, including leptospirosis and rabies, which may be passed to humans. Rabid skunks are often very active and aggressive. The virus is present in their saliva, so animals and humans only catch the disease if they are bitten.

Humans are responsible for many skunk deaths, including trapping for the fur trade. Skunks are also killed by vehicles, since they are attracted to roads when searching for carrion.

⊕ *A striped skunk digs for worms and grubs, its favorite food in a largely insectivorous diet.*

long periods in underground burrows, often made by woodchucks or badgers. Some skunks dig their own burrows, but they are not very long or deep. During winter striped skunks will den alone or together in groups of up to 20 animals. Communal denning is more common in the colder, more northerly parts of their range. It seems that skunks will overcome their usual dislike of company to take advantage of the warmth of many bodies. Striped skunks

Skunks at Your Service

Although skunks usually have a bad reputation, they probably do more good than harm. They eat a huge number of agricultural pests, such as armyworms, cutworms, Colorado potato beetles, grasshoppers, beetle grubs, and squash bugs. They are also good at catching mice and rats. Skunks save farmers a lot of money in terms of the amount of pesticides that would be needed if the hungry skunks were not there.

The Civet and Genet Family

Civets and genets are small- to medium-sized animals with a catlike appearance. The family Viverridae (civets, genets, and linsangs) and the Herpestidae (mongooses) are similar to an ancestral carnivorous mammalian group, the Miacoidea, that lived in the Eocene period, about 56 to 35 million years ago. Miacoidea fossils show many similarities to the skeleton and tooth structure of modern viverrids and herpestids.

Family Viverridae: 6 subfamilies, 20 genera, 35 species

AFRICAN PALM CIVET 1 genus, 1 species
Nandinia African palm civet (*N. binotata*)

PALM CIVETS 5 genera, 7 species
Arctogalidia 1 species, small-toothed palm civet (*A. trivirgata*)
Paradoxurus 3 species, common palm civet (*P. hermaphroditus*); golden palm civet (*P. zeylonensis*); Jerdon's palm civet (*P. jerdoni*)
Paguma 1 species, masked palm civet (*P. larvata*)
Macrogalidia 1 species, Sulawesi palm civet (*M. musschenbroekii*)
Arctictis 1 species, binturong (*A. binturong*)

BANDED PALM CIVETS 4 genera, 5 species
Hemigalus 1 species, banded palm civet (*H. derbyanus*)
Diplogale 1 species, Hose's palm civet (*D. hosei*)
Chrotogale 1 species, Owston's banded civet (*C. owstoni*)
Cynogale 2 species, otter civet (*C. bennettii*); Lowe's otter civet (*C. lowei*)

TRUE CIVETS, LINSANGS, AND GENETS 7 genera, 19 species
Poiana 1 species, African linsang (*P. richardsoni*)
Prionodon 2 species, spotted linsang (*P. pardicolor*); banded linsang (*P. linsang*)
Viverricula 1 species, small Indian civet (*V. indica*)
Viverra 3 species, Oriental or Malayan civet (*V. tangalunga*); large Indian civet (*V. zibetha*); large spotted civet (*V. megaspila*)
Civettictis 1 species, African civet (*C. civetta*)
Osbornictis 1 species, aquatic genet (*O. piscivora*)
Genetta 10 species, including common genet (*G. genetta*); large-spotted genet (*G. tigrina*)

MALAGASY CIVETS 2 genera, 2 species
Eupleres 1 species, falanouc (*E. goudotii*)
Fossa 1 species, fanaloka (*F. fossa*)

FOSSA 1 genus, 1 species
Cryptoprocta fossa (*C. ferox*)

What Is a Civet?

Civets, genets, and linsangs are the closest relatives of the cat family. However, although they are similar to cats in many ways, there are also a number of differences. Civets and their relatives have long bodies and relatively short legs compared with cats. They also have a longer, more pointed head and face than their feline relatives. Many of the differences between viverrids and cats are linked to their lifestyles. Cats rely totally on hunting animal prey for food, while civets and genets take more vegetable food, so are less specialized killers. Cats have short, strong jaws for gripping struggling prey, large canine teeth, and large, powerful claws. Civets and genets have more slender, weaker jaws, comparatively small canine teeth, and shorter, less powerful claws.

A civet's coat is generally sandy gray with dark spots or stripes. The tail is usually marked with bands or is a different color than the rest of the body. Some species, such as the binturong, have a coat of a single color. The masked palm civet is uniform in color except for markings on its face. Some civet and genet species are armed with stink glands. When in danger, they are able to spray a stream of vile yellow fluid at an attacker. The liquid is nauseating and repellent, and may temporarily blind or cause discomfort to the attacker, so giving the intended victim a chance to escape. It may be that some of the bold coat markings found in civets serve as a warning to predators, like the distinctive patterns of a skunk, discouraging them from making an attack. In other species the markings help break up the outline of the animal, protecting it by camouflage. It is important

 SEE ALSO Skunk, Striped **1**:84; Genet, Common **1**:92; Civet, Common Palm **1**:94; Fossa **1**:96; Mongoose Family, The **1**:98

⊕ *A binturong forages for fruit in a tree. The binturong is a tree-dwelling species with a strong tail, which it uses to hold onto branches while picking fruit with its paws.*

for civets and genets to have such defenses because, although they are hunters themselves, they are also targets for larger predators.

Different species of viverrid have different lifestyles and types of prey. Hence there is a range of body forms within the family. Although all species are good climbers, some—such as the true civets—rarely climb trees to find food. Such species tend to have feet with well-padded soles that are covered with hairs. Their paws are small and compact, and they only walk on their toes. Tree-dwelling species generally have broad feet with bare soles, a factor that improves their grip when climbing. They use the whole of the foot when walking, like a bear, and use all the toes to get a better grip. Feet also vary depending on the type of food taken by a species. Linsangs, like cats, live almost entirely on animals they kill themselves and—like cats—have fully retractile claws with protective sheaths. Species that eat a greater variety of food have feet that are less specialized for prey taking. The form of the teeth also varies between species. The meat-eating linsang's molar teeth are sharp and bladelike, similar to those of cats. True civets eat both meat and

→ *Some members of the civet family shown in characteristic activities: African linsang feeding on a nestling (1); banded palm civet eating a lizard (2); Oriental or Malayan civet (3); common palm civet scenting the air (4); binturong foraging for fruit while grasping a branch with its prehensile tail (5).*

vegetable matter, and have broad-crowned molar teeth that are suitable both for cutting and grinding food. The palm civets take mostly vegetable food. Their molars are even broader, making them less suitable for chewing meat but better for grinding up vegetable matter.

Unlike cats, which have rough tongues that they use to lick bones clean, civets and genets have smooth tongues, like dogs. This is because—in the same way as dogs—they crush and swallow the bones of their prey and so do not need to lick the bones clean. The form of the skull also varies between species: Genets have catlike skulls, while the skulls of civets are more heavily built. Palm civets have comparatively sturdy skulls.

Where Civets and Genets Live

The largest number of viverrid species are found in India and the Malay Peninsula. True civet fossils have been discovered in a cave in Madras, southern India, and also in the rocks of the Siwalik Hills in northern India, providing evidence that they have lived in this region since prehistoric times. Today members of the family are found throughout most of Africa, India, and Southeast Asia to Borneo and the Philippines. Some also occur in southwestern Europe, the Near East, and the Arabian Peninsula. There are no civets or genets in the Americas.

The island of Madagascar is home to three unusual species that are found nowhere else, including the pantherlike fossa. Palm civets and banded palm civets are generally Asian, although there is one African species. The true civets are mostly confined to Asia. Linsangs are found in both Africa and Asia. Genets are found only in Africa, but one species occurs in southwestern Europe.

Most species of civets and genets live in forested areas. They are found from rain forests to woodlands, in woody scrub, and occasionally in savanna. Only two species of civet manage to live in dry open country—the small Indian civet and the common palm civet. Some species will live on mountains up to a height of

Civet Oil

Civets and genets are probably best known as the source of civet (or musk) oil, a scent used in making perfume. The word "civet" actually comes from the Arabic word *zabad* for the scented liquid that issues from the glands of most viverrids. Genet scent has a subtle, pleasing smell, but true civet species, such as the African, large Indian, and small Indian civets, are the ones used in the commercial perfume industry. The fluid, collected from captive animals, is a clear, yellowish-brown mixture of fats and oils. The original oil has an offensive smell to humans, but becomes a pleasant scent when purified and diluted. The use of civet oil in perfume dates back at least to the 10th century B.C., when it was imported from Africa by King Solomon. Civet oil is believed to have medicinal properties and has been used as a cure for sweating and certain skin conditions. The development of synthetic substitutes has reduced the need for civet oil, but East African and Asian countries still export large quantities.

Civets and genets use their pungent secretions for scent marking. The process is the most important means of communication between these solitary animals. It is used to define territories and by males during the breeding season to attract females.

All civets and genets are good climbers, but there are both tree- and ground-dwelling species. Palm civets are mainly tree dwelling and are skillful climbers that use their semiretractile claws for extra grip. The binturong, a species of palm civet, even has a prehensile tail (capable of grasping), which it uses to hold onto branches while picking fruit with its paws. The diet of palm civets largely consists of fruit, but they also take animal prey. Banded palm civets spend less time in the trees and are generally more carnivorous, foraging on the ground and in the trees at night for invertebrates, small lizards, and mammals. Owston's banded civet takes almost entirely invertebrate prey. The true civets are a highly varied group, but the majority of them are ground dwelling and generally more doglike than other viverrids.

In Africa genets occur in all habitats except desert and are particularly adapted to living in the trees. Apart from the aquatic genet, they all have dark rows of spots or stripes along their bodies. Like the linsangs, the genets are almost all carnivorous and have fully retractile claws. Linsangs are some of the rarest members of the Viverridae. There are three species, and all are small, secretive animals found only in forested areas.

There are also some aquatic species of civet, such as otter civets. They have smaller ears, a blunter muzzle, a more compact body, and shorter tails than other civets. While resembling otters in body form, their toes are less webbed, and they are still good at climbing.

7,000 feet (2,100 m). In cold places they grow a thick coat for the winter. Most species forage and hunt for food at night and spend the day in a rock crevice, burrow, or hollow tree. Some species, such as the linsangs, may even build themselves nests up in the branches.

Lifestyle

Most species of civet and genet live alone. Males and females come together briefly during the breeding season; but once mating has taken place, they separate, and the female raises the young on her own. An exception to the rule is the Madagascan fanaloka, which lives in pairs.

⊖ *The fossa has a catlike head and retractile claws for capturing prey (1). Also shown here are the mongooselike falanouc (2) and the foxlike Madagascan fanaloka (3).*

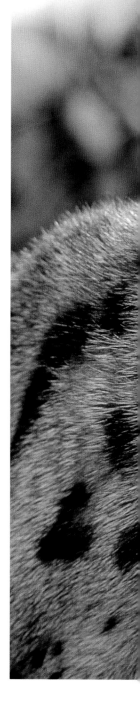

Common name
Common genet
(European or small-
spotted genet)

Scientific name *Genetta genetta*

Family Viverridae

Order Carnivora

Size Length head/body: 16–22 in
(40–55 cm); tail length: 16–20 in
(40–50 cm); height at shoulder:
7–8 in (18–20 cm)

Weight 3–5 lb (1.5–2 kg)

Key features Sandy coat with dark spots forming long
stripes; tail with dark rings and white tip;
short, dark crest of longer hair down spine

Habits Active during the night and twilight periods;
solitary, but tolerates meetings with others;
climbs, jumps, and swims well

Breeding Litters of 1–4 young born after gestation
period of 70 days. Breeding occurs year-
round, but mainly April to May and August to
September. Weaned at 6 months; sexually
mature at 2 years. May live up to 20 years in
captivity, probably many fewer in the wild

Voice Normally silent, but will hiss, growl, purr, and
mew; may also cough, whine, or scream

Diet Mostly rodents, especially mice; also rabbits,
birds, lizards, fruit, berries, and insects

Habitat Dense scrub, woodland, and rocky areas; up
to 6,500 ft (2,000 m) in the Pyrenees

Distribution Europe (France and the Iberian Peninsula),
Palestine, and Africa (except for the Sahara
Desert and Congo River Basin)

Status Population: abundant; IUCN Vulnerable
(Balearic Island subspecies). Widespread and
fairly common

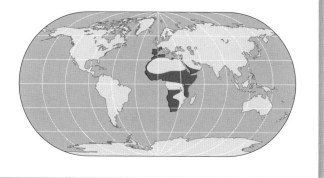

Common Genet

Genetta genetta

*The common genet is the only species of genet found
outside Africa. Individuals were kept as pets by the
ancient Greeks and Romans before the domestic cat
became popular.*

GENETS ARE LONG, THIN CATLIKE animals with
pointed muzzles. As well as being the only
species of genet outside Africa, the common
genet is also the most widespread genet in
Africa. It is found in almost all regions except
the Sahara Desert and dense forests of the
Congo River Basin. The species may originally
have reached southern Europe by crossing the
land bridge that once connected Gibraltar on
the southern tip of Spain with Morocco in
North Africa. It may also have been intentionally
introduced to Europe by humans in the Middle
Ages. The common genets on the Balearic
Islands were definitely taken there by people.
Today common genets are still found in Europe,
but only in the southwest. At one time they
occurred as far north as Belgium and Germany.

Creatures of the Night
Common genets are nocturnal, being active at
dawn, dusk, and most of the night. They usually
rest at some point during the hours of darkness
and will occasionally be inactive in the early
morning. They spend their days tucked away in
rock crevices or burrows dug by other animals.
Alternatively, they may use tree hollows or
sometimes large branches. They often use the
same shelter day after day for long periods.

Male genets have home ranges of up to
2 square miles (5 sq. km) in size. The ranges of
females tend to be much smaller, and a male's
range may overlap the ranges of several
females. Latrines and scent-marking sites are
used by more than one individual. Genets are
solitary animals, but they sometimes travel in
pairs, particularly during the breeding season.

at about eight weeks and to take solid food at the same time. By six months they are fully weaned and become independent from their mother at one year.

Seasonal Diet

The diet of common genets consists of any small animals they can catch, and varies with region depending on what animals are common locally. In Africa genets feed mainly on small mammals such as rodents. In Spain they also take a lot of lizards; and although they eat some rodents all year round, birds make up half their diet in the spring and summer months. Genets also eat fruit, mainly in the fall and winter. Genets are stealthy hunters, relying on speed and agility to catch their prey. Their coat markings of spots and stripes help disguise their shape, enabling them to sneak up on other animals. They crouch down low until their body and tail appear to be gliding across the ground—and pounce with a lightning strike.

⬅ *As well as foraging and hunting on the ground, the genet is a skillful climber and can catch nesting and roosting birds in the branches of trees.*

Genets are good mouse and rat catchers, and those living near human habitation can help control troublesome rodents. As pets they share similar characteristics with cats and were kept both for their ability to catch vermin and for their affectionate nature toward their owners. There are records showing that tame genets were common in Constantinople when it was part of the Roman Empire.

Meetings between genets are rarely aggressive.

Most breeding takes place during April and May or August and September. Females in captivity are able to produce two litters a year. At birth the young measure about 5 inches (13.5 cm) long and weigh between 2 and 3 ounces (61 and 82 g). They are born blind, but their eyes begin to open after eight days. They start to leave their tree nest or burrow

The common genet is widespread on two continents and generally abundant, but there are areas within its geographical range where local populations are threatened. In particular, its numbers in Europe have declined owing to persecution: On the Balearic Island of Ibiza the common genet is listed as Vulnerable by the IUCN. Common genets are often blamed for attacks on game birds and poultry. In addition, they are hunted for their luxuriant winter coats.

Common name Common palm civet (toddy cat)

Scientific name *Paradoxurus hermaphroditus*

Family Viverridae

Order Carnivora

Size Length head/body: 16.5–27.5 in (42–70 cm); tail length: 16–24 in (41–60 cm)

Weight 6–10 lb (2.7–4.5 kg)

Key features Sandy gray to dark-brown coat with black stripes down back; spots on shoulders, sides, and base of tail; face has mask of spots and a streak on the forehead; tail tip may be white

Habits Nocturnal; expert climber; spends much time in trees

Breeding Litters of 2–5 young born mainly between October and December after gestation period of 3 months. Weaned at 6 months; sexually mature at 11–12 months. May live up to 25 years in captivity, about 10 in the wild

Voice Normally silent

Diet Small vertebrates such as mice and lizards; also insects, fruit, and seeds

Habitat Forests and wooded areas; may shelter in thatched roofs and pipes

Distribution Kashmir, Indian Peninsula, and Sri Lanka to southeastern China and Malay Peninsula; also islands of Hainan (China), Sumatra, Sulawesi, Simeulue, Enggano, Kangean Islands, Java (Indonesia), Palawan (Philippines), Borneo, and many other nearby islands

Status Population: abundant; IUCN Vulnerable (subspecies *P. h. lignicolor*). A common animal

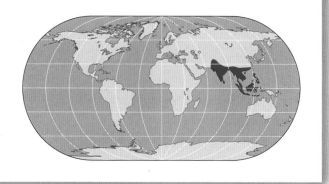

 SEE ALSO Genet, Common **1**:92; Fossa **1**:96

Common Palm Civet

Paradoxurus hermaphroditus

The fruit-eating common palm civet is also known as the toddy cat because of its habit of raiding plantations in search of the sweet sap of palm trees, which ferments to make a mildly alcoholic "toddy."

THE COMMON PALM CIVET IS one of the most widespread species of palm civets. It spends less time in trees than most other species of palm civet. Instead, it forages on the ground for fallen fruit and small animals. It is only active at night and spends the day curled up in the branches of a tree or the hollow of a trunk. The Latin name, *Paradoxurus hermaphroditus*, reflects the fact that the species is a puzzle to scientists and difficult to sex. A hermaphrodite is an animal that has both male and female genitalia. The reason why the two sexes are often confused in the common palm civet is that the scent gland, located near the genitals, can make a male animal look like a female.

Palm civets are solitary animals, and a female will only tolerate a male in her tree during the breeding season. Mating takes place in June. Dominant male palm civets have large territories that overlap the living space of a number of female palm civets, but they will generally allow smaller, immature, or elderly males to be present. However, when a young male matures, he is a threat to the dominant male's right to the females in the area. A fight usually determines which of the two males will keep the territory. Dominant males patrol their ranges, covering the whole area at least once every five to 10 days.

Sowing the Seeds

Although they take some animal prey, palm civets eat a wide variety of fruit. For example, in Java the common palm civet eats the fruit of at least 35 different trees, palms, shrubs, and vines. When fruit is eaten, the hard seeds are not digested, but travel through the animal's gut to be passed out in its droppings. Not only does this allow the seeds to be carried far away from the parent plant, it also provides them with some nice compost to grow in. Along with other forest-dwelling mammals, palm civets therefore play an important role in the dispersal of tropical forest seeds.

Common palm civets sometimes eat fruit that would be harmful to humans, but do not appear to be adversely affected: They eat the seeds of the Arenga palm in large quantities, even though they have a prickly outer pulp. Laborers on coffee plantations watch out for the piles of droppings left by palm civets that have been feeding on coffee berries: They may recover the beans from the droppings to add them to their store for market.

Large mango or palm trees found close to human settlements provide good daytime shelter for palm civets. However, some common palm civets go a step further and make their homes in house roofs, under floorboards, and in drains—even in the center of crowded cities.

⊕ Newborn palm civets weigh 2.5 to 3.5 ounces (70 to 100 g). Juvenile males leave their mother shortly after they are weaned, while young females share their mother's territory until they are two years old.

Such individuals become very accustomed to people and often quite tame and affectionate. Occasionally, palm civets are even kept as pets. People have also taken common palm civets to a number of islands to use as rat catchers, perhaps explaining how they arrived on many Southeast Asian islands, such as the Philippines and Sulawesi.

Toddy Cat

Some common palm civets have become almost parasitic on humans. Having been tempted into towns and villages by the abundance of rats and mice, they unfortunately do not stick to rodent prey, but learn to take poultry and raid crops. All palm civets are well-known banana thieves, and common palm civets are particularly fond of pineapple. In some areas palm trees are tapped for palm sap, or "toddy," from which alcoholic drinks such as the spirit arak are made. Common palm civets climb the tapped tree to steal the sweet liquid that collects overnight in jars. It is such behavior that gives common palm civets their other name of "toddy cat" and makes them unpopular in areas where palms are used for such purposes.

Common name Fossa

Scientific name *Cryptoprocta ferox*

Family Viverridae

Order Carnivora

Size Length head/body: 24–31 in (60–80 cm); tail length: 24–30 in (60–75 cm); height at shoulder: 14 in (35 cm)

Weight 15–26 lb (7–12 kg); occasionally up to 44 lb (20 kg)

Key features Reddish-brown to dark-brown coat, occasionally black; fur is short, thick, and smooth; catlike head with rounded ears; feet are webbed and have short, retractile claws

Habits Mainly nocturnal, but can be active in daylight; lives mostly in trees and is a skilled climber and powerful predator; solitary except during the breeding season

Breeding Litters of 2–4 young born after gestation period of 3 months. Weaned at 4–6 months; sexually mature at 4 years. May live to at least 20 years in captivity, probably fewer in the wild

Voice Generally silent

Diet Lemurs, small mammals, and birds; also reptiles, frogs, snakes, and insects

Habitat Rain forest and wooded savanna

Distribution Madagascar

Status Population: probably only a few hundred; IUCN Endangered; CITES II

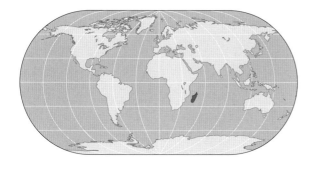

Fossa

Cryptoprocta ferox

The fossa resembles a short-legged, dwarf puma. It is a powerful predator and has a fierce reputation in its native Madagascar. Lemurs provide much of its diet— a testament to its formidable hunting skills.

THE FOSSA'S MANY SIMILARITIES with cats, including its strong predatory nature, meant that in the past it was often classified in the cat family— the Felidae. It is similar to a small puma, but has a longer head in relation to its body than typical members of the cat family. Fossas have catlike claws, but unlike true cats—which walk on their toes—fossas walk flat-footed like bears. Sometimes the fossa is placed in the mongoose family, reflecting similarities with that group, too. The general view, however, is that the fossa is a civet that lives like a cat. Hence it is classified as a rather special member of the family Viverridae. Perhaps its distinctiveness is a result of long isolation on the island of Madagascar, allowing the species to evolve into something different from its ancestors on the African mainland.

Top Island Predator

Fossas are the top predators in Madagascar and have no natural enemies apart from people. They are also Madagascar's largest land mammal. Fossas are more agile in trees than cats. They can run down a trunk headfirst and jump about 6 feet (2 m) between trees. They need to be excellent climbers in order to catch the lemurs (the primitive primates of the Madagascan forests) that make up more than half their diet. It is very unusual for primates to feature regularly in the diet of any animal, since they are generally smarter and much better climbers than most predator species. The fact that lemurs are often part of a fossa's diet shows what an agile and skillful hunter it is.

Fossas are as at home on the ground as they are in the trees and have been known to steal chickens and sheep, and take small wild

⊕ *Despite being a ferocious predator, the fossa is now a threatened species, largely due to forest clearance. A single animal occupies an area of 4 to 8 square miles (10 to 20 sq. km), and destruction of its habitat is leaving forest areas too small to support secure populations.*

 SEE ALSO Mongoose Family, The **1**:98; Puma **2**:42; Lemur, Ringtailed **4**:98; Lemur, Ruffed **4**:104

pigs. The native people of Madagascar consider the fossa to be a dangerous and ferocious chicken thief, and known offenders are often shot on sight. When local people spend the night in the forests, they will often keep a fire going throughout the hours of darkness because they are frightened of being attacked by a fossa while they are sleeping.

Although fossas occasionally raid human camps for food, they do so very discreetly, often not even waking guard dogs. The fossa's reputation as a dangerous animal is greatly exaggerated, and it will usually flee at the first sight of a human.

The mating behavior of fossas is different from that of other viverrids, which usually mate with the one or two animals that have territories overlapping their own: A female fossa will spend several days high in a tree, during which time a number of males group together beneath it and call up to the female. She will allow several males to visit her one at a time for mating. About a week later a new female will arrive at the tree to mate with the males there, and the resident female will leave.

Unusual Puberty

During puberty the female fossa goes through a strange stage of sexual development: The clitoris becomes large and develops a small supporting bone and a covering of spines—similar to the male penis. Also, the creamy-colored underparts become covered by a bright orange liquid that is usually only released by the male. It is not known why females go through this "masculine" period, and it may simply be a side effect of the hormonal changes that occur during puberty.

The fossa is now officially listed as Endangered by the IUCN. The destruction of its homeland through forest clearance poses the greatest threat to its survival.

⊕ *A fossa leaps between trees while hunting lemurs. Fossas share characteristics with cats, but are more agile in trees. They are able to catch and kill lemurs, despite those animals being intelligent and capable creatures.*

The Mongoose Family

Mongooses are extremely similar in form to the early carnivores, the Miacoidea. They are active and agile terrestrial mammals that live either in groups or alone. With the exception of recent introductions, mongooses are restricted to the Old World (Eastern Hemisphere, excluding Australasia). Some species have been released in other areas of the world, including the West Indies, Fiji, and the Hawaiian Islands in attempts to control local vermin, such as rats and snakes.

Family Herpestidae: 2 subfamilies, 17 genera, 35 species

AFRICAN AND ASIAN MONGOOSES AND MEERKATS 13 genera, 30 species

Atilax 1 species, marsh mongoose (*A. paludinosus*)

Bdeogale 3 species, including bushy-tailed mongoose (*B. crassicauda*); Jackson's mongoose (*B. jacksoni*)

Crossarchus 3 species, including Alexander's mongoose (*C. alexandri*); Angolan mongoose (*C. ansorgei*)

Cynictis 1 species, yellow mongoose (*C. penicillata*)

Dologale 1 species, Pousargues' mongoose (*D. dybowskii*)

Helogale 1 species, dwarf mongoose (*H. parvula*)

Herpestes 13 species, including Egyptian mongoose (*H. ichneumon*); long-nosed mongoose (*H. naso*)

Rhynchogale 1 species, Meller's mongoose (*R. melleri*)

Liberiictis 1 species, Liberian mongoose (*L. kuhni*)

Mungos 2 species, Gambian mongoose (*M. gambianus*); banded mongoose (*M. mungo*)

Ichneumia 1 species, white-tailed mongoose (*I. albicauda*)

Paracynictis 1 species, Selous' mongoose (*P. selousi*)

Suricata 1 species, meerkat (*S. suricatta*)

MALAGASY MONGOOSES 4 genera, 5 species

Galidia 1 species, ringtailed mongoose (*G. elegans*)

Galidictis 2 species, broad-striped mongoose (*G. fasciata*); giant-striped mongoose (*G. grandidieri*)

Mungotictis 1 species, narrow-striped mongoose (*M. decemlineata*)

Salanoia 1 species, brown mongoose (*S. concolor*)

What Is a Mongoose?

Mongooses are long, thin creatures with a pointed face, small, rounded ears, and a tapering, bushy tail of about half to three-quarters the length of the body. Their legs are short, and the paws have long, nonretractile claws. The smallest species, the dwarf mongoose, has a total length of about 17 inches (43 cm) and weighs just 11 ounces (312 g). The largest species, the white-tailed mongoose, measures 40 inches (102 cm) and weighs 11 pounds (5 kg).

The mongoose family is closely related to the civet and genet family. They are sometimes all classified as the same family, the Viverridae. Mongooses differ from civets and genets in that they possess nonretractile claws, rounded ears that rarely stick out above the profile of the head, four or five toes on each foot, and little or no webbing between their toes. They also differ in their behavior. Civets and genets are generally tree dwelling, nocturnal, and solitary. Mongooses, however, tend to remain on the ground and can be active during either the day or night, depending on the species. Some species are social and live in large family groups.

Mongoose fur is long, coarse, and generally brindled or grizzled (where the individual hairs are colored differently along their length). A few species, such as the meerkat and banded mongoose, have bands across their back, and two Madagascan species have stripes that run the length of their body. No mongooses have spots, but legs, feet, and tail or tail tip may be a different color from the rest of the body. Some species have different color forms depending on where they live. For example, the slender mongoose is usually gray to yellowish brown, but in the Kalahari Desert in southern Africa it is red, and in some areas a black form is found. Such variations usually match the soil color of the area and may be important in making the animals less obvious to predators.

 SEE ALSO Civet and Genet Family, The **1**:88; Meerkat **1**:100; Mongoose, Dwarf **1**:106; Mongoose, Banded **1**:110

→ *Some mongoose species: bushy-tailed mongoose—Kenyan subspecies, sniffing the air in a typical mongoose posture (1); white-tailed mongoose (2); ringtailed mongoose (3); dwarf mongoose adult feeding a beetle to a juvenile (4); narrow-striped mongoose (5); Selous' mongoose (6); Egyptian mongoose with an egg (7); marsh mongoose (8).*

Mongooses have a phenomenal sense of smell, and they mark their territories with scent. Social species mark each other in the same way to help recognize members of the group. Scents are produced both by cheek and anal glands. Scents will communicate the individual identity of the marker, as well as its sex and breeding condition. A mongoose's eyesight is also generally good; and unlike most mammals, which only have partial color vision, it is able to see color.

Although mongooses are carnivores, they will also eat vegetable matter, such as fruit. The canine and carnassial teeth (those adapted for shearing flesh) are relatively small for a carnivorous animal, probably owing to the number of invertebrates and small animals in the diet, which make carnassials unnecessary. The mongoose skull has a long facial section and is generally more robust than a genet skull.

Where Mongooses Live

The mongoose family is split between group-living and solitary species. The social species also tend to be the smaller ones, such as the dwarf mongoose and meerkat. They use safety in numbers as protection against predators. Group-living species tend to be active during the day, while solitary species are usually nocturnal, using the cover of night as a defense.

Mongoose habitat varies greatly between species. In general, solitary species tend to inhabit wooded and forested areas, while social species prefer open plains. For group-living species, den sites rather than habitat may determine where the animals live. On African grasslands, where the soil is hard and unsuitable for digging, termite mounds provide a good alternative to burrows. The presence of mongooses here may depend on the availability of mounds. Most species are terrestrial, but some are semiaquatic or tree dwelling. Mongooses are opportunist feeders and take a wide variety of prey from small insects to full-size cobras. They may also eat eggs and fruit. Species living in dry areas can obtain water by chewing wild melons and digging up roots. The smaller, communal species, such as the dwarf mongoose and meerkat, forage in groups and tend to feed mainly on invertebrates, lizards, and small rodents. Larger species are usually solitary and feed mainly on larger prey.

Meerkat

Suricata suricatta

A meerkat sentry is a familiar sight on the southern African savanna, demonstrating the selfless and cooperative behavior of this plucky mongoose species toward members of its own pack.

Common name Meerkat (suricate, gray meerkat, slender-tailed meerkat)

Scientific name *Suricata suricatta*

Family Herpestidae

Order Carnivora

Size Length head/body: 12–18 in (30–45 cm); tail length: 6–12 in (15–30 cm); height at shoulder: 4 in (10 cm)

Weight 3.3–5 lb (1.5–2.3 kg)

Key features Slender, short-legged animal; tan to gray with broken brown bands on back and sides; black eye rings, ears, and tail tip

Habits Social: lives in colonies of up to 30, but usually 10–15, animals; sentries posted to watch for predators while colony is foraging

Breeding Two to 5 young born after gestation period of 75 days. Weaned at 9–10 weeks; sexually mature at about 12 months. May live 13 years in captivity, up to 10 in the wild, but more commonly 6

Voice A variety of chirrups, trills, growls, and barks

Diet Insects, scorpions, and grubs; occasionally lizards, small snakes, birds, and mice

Habitat Dry savanna, open plains, and scrubland

Distribution Southern Africa in Angola, Namibia, South Africa, and southern Botswana

Status Population: abundant. Not threatened, but numbers have fallen in some areas

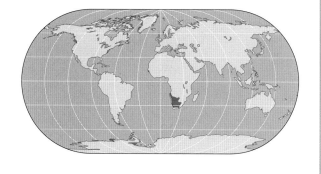

MEERKATS ARE THE MOST SOCIABLE members of the mongoose family. They live in packs, which may include several breeding pairs. The female of a breeding pair may be larger than the male and may dominate him. However, no distinct hierarchies have been observed in meerkat packs, and group members are rarely aggressive toward each other. All group members take part in the various tasks involved in pack life, such as baby-sitting, tunnel maintenance, and sentry duty. Both females and males without young of their own will help guard and provide food for other meerkats' young. Some females will produce milk even if they have not been pregnant and will suckle other females' babies.

Juvenile Followers

Meerkats breed throughout the year, but most births occur during the warmer, wetter months. Young meerkats begin to take adult food when they are about three to four weeks old. Toward the end of weaning the young begin to follow the rest of the group. While adult meerkats are reluctant to share food with each other, they will often give food to juvenile members of the group, even if they are not their own offspring. Each youngster will associate itself with a particular adult and follow it around, begging food from it. The adult will pass on its best-quality prey to its follower, who will not only be fed, but will also learn how to behave as a meerkat. When the young start following, the juvenile meerkats from earlier litters may get confused between begging for food from adults and giving food to the new arrivals: Adolescent meerkats have been seen to beg food from an adult only to pass it onto young from the next litter, or to give food to a youngster, then steal it back again. Meerkat life is complicated, but also highly social.

Meerkats have strong, muscular forelimbs with large claws, which make them excellent diggers. Their long, slender, short-legged bodies are perfect for traveling inside underground tunnels. Although they are quite capable of digging their own burrows (or warrens), meerkats often share dens with African ground squirrels or yellow mongooses. In such cases the dens are usually dug by the ground squirrels, and the meerkats move in later. Neither species appears to object to the presence of the other—in fact, the meerkats ignore the ground squirrels altogether.

Underground Refuge

Meerkat warrens typically cover an area about 16 feet (5 m) across and, depending on ground conditions, may have up to three levels, with the deepest tunnels about 10 feet (3 m) below the surface. The largest warrens may have up to 90 entrances, but about 15 entrance holes are more usual. Within the warren a series of tunnels connects chambers of about 12 inches (30 cm) across. Meerkats usually stay within easy reach of a warren, which is their main refuge from predators. The temperature in deeper tunnels may vary by only a degree or two, making the warrens important shelters from the extreme desert temperatures above ground. Meerkats spend nighttime within their warrens—the coldest parts of winter days and the hottest parts of summer days are spent inside too. The territory of a meerkat group may be up to 6 square miles (15 sq. km) and will contain five or six warrens, occupied in rotation. Meerkats spend from a few days to several months around one warren, moving on when the surrounding food supply has been used up.

A meerkat pack is very protective of its territory. Marking of territories using scent from

⊖ *A male meerkat on guard duty in the Kalahari Desert, southern Africa. Sentries are posted in high places to watch out for predators while the group is foraging.*

101

Dicing with Death

Meerkats will take on venomous snakes much larger than themselves—either as a potential source of food or in order to rid their den sites of lurking predators. Members of the mongoose family in general have a higher resistance to snake venom than humans, and meerkats are no exception. However, it is the speed and skill of their attack that usually prevents the animals from getting bitten. Meerkats are also particularly fond of scorpions and can withstand stings strong enough to kill a human being.

the anal glands is generally performed by the males. If a rival pack is spotted entering the territory, it will first be approached in a threatening manner. If the threat does not discourage the trespassing group, the two packs may end up in a fight, often led by the largest male. All members of the pack except the young will take part. Once the fight is won or lost, the two packs separate. Low-ranking males from the winning side may take the opportunity to improve their breeding status by chasing off the losing males and taking over both their territory and their females.

Takeover Bids

All meerkats reaching maturity within a group have the problem of establishing themselves as breeding animals. Some males may form bachelor groups that roam around without a territory, sometimes attacking established packs in an attempt to drive out the resident males and take over their females.

Young female meerkats may also group together to leave their parent pack, often meeting up with bachelor male groups and forming packs of their own. Dominant females may try to stop the young females from leaving, since they do not want to lose their helpful baby-sitters. Females may also try to join an established group, although it may take a long

time to be accepted. One lone female followed a pack for two weeks until an established female gave birth, and the lone female was taken on as a baby-sitter. She was forced to continue her role for several weeks, with little time for foraging, before attacks on her became less severe, and she was fully accepted into the pack.

Safety in Numbers

Meerkats take a different foraging route every day. They usually allow about a week before returning to an area to enable their food sources to be replenished. The clawed muscular front arms are used to dig out prey and to hold larger animals, such as lizards and mice. Like other social mongooses, meerkats feed as a group, but spread out to forage and do not cooperate in looking for food. The group provides protection against predators; but since the meerkats' own prey is small, there is no point in hunting together in order to bring down large animals. There are some exceptions, however. For example, if a meerkat gets the scent of a large gecko, it will accept the help of another animal to dig the lizard out of its burrow. Although it may take half an hour to uncover the gecko, the effort is worthwhile,

⊖ Meerkats take part in the communal digging of a den. Although meerkats are quite capable of digging their own dens, they often move into dens dug by African ground squirrels. Neither animal seems to mind the communal living arrangement.

since geckoes are big and often live in pairs. The meerkats will cooperate in this situation since each is guaranteed a good meal.

Foraging in a group reduces the danger of any one meerkat being caught by a predator, since it is more likely an attacker will be spotted by a group of meerkats than by a single animal. Safety is further improved since guards are posted in high places to keep watch over the foraging group. When it spots a predator, the sentry gives an alarm call that tells the rest of the pack to run for cover. Meerkats cannot concentrate on foraging and watch for predators at the same time. Therefore the more time a meerkat spends looking out for predators, the less time will be available for feeding. By foraging in a group, individual animals can find more food and will be healthier than animals foraging alone.

Sentry Duty

By performing guard duty, a sentry meerkat is sacrificing valuable feeding time. Its position on high points, such as rocks or bushes, also exposes it to danger from predators and heat stroke. Being a sentry is a job done on behalf of the group, but the animals take turns and share the risk. Meerkats that remain behind baby-sitting young at the den will not leave to feed themselves. Since many members of the meerkat team perform such "selfless" tasks, it could encourage an individual to take advantage of the help given by others. However, such behavior is not tolerated in a meerkat pack. For example, it was observed that during a fight with a rival pack a female member of a meerkat group was seen lazing in the shade rather than helping her companions. After the pack had chased off the intruders, they turned on the idle female—seemingly as a punishment for her selfish behavior.

As well as foraging in a group and having sentries, meerkats have other antipredator defenses. Like the banded mongoose, meerkats make mob attacks against animals that are potential threats—such as snakes and jackals. In encounters with predators or other meerkat gangs individuals make themselves look more imposing by raising their tails vertically, arching their backs, making their hair stand on end, and growling and spitting like a cat. If the meerkat's tactics do not work and it is threatened by a predator, it will take up the classic mongoose defense position: It will throw itself on its back, so protecting the sensitive nape of the neck, with teeth and claws facing the predator. The

⊕ *A meerkat "helper" acts as a baby-sitter for young animals. Meerkats are the most social of the mongooses, and members of the pack will take turns performing group duties such as baby-sitting and tunnel maintenance.*

bushy tail with hairs standing up may be placed over the belly and head. An attack from the sky by an eagle or hawk causes the meerkats to run for cover. If a pack is attacked in the open, away from their warren, the adults will throw themselves over the juvenile members of the pack to protect them. Like banded mongooses, if a member of the pack is captured, the others will launch a rescue attempt.

Nursing Care

If a member of the pack is left injured after an attack, it may be nursed back to health by the other members. A female meerkat that had been caught and injured by an eagle was observed being surrounded by her pack and helped back to the warren. The female had produced a litter of kittens a few days earlier and was left with them in the burrow while the rest of the pack went to forage. She was fed with grubs by the other members of her pack and was also helped to stand upright during the morning sunbathing session. Thanks to the support of the group both the female and her litter survived. Invalid care is only performed for adult meerkats, since the loss of a baby is less damaging to the group than that of an adult.

⊙ *A meerkat group basks in the morning sunshine. Meerkats need to sunbathe each day to keep themselves at the correct body temperature.*

Sun Worshipping

Along with underground dens and group nesting, sunbathing plays an important part in keeping meerkats at their correct body temperature. When they leave the burrow, members sit or stand in an upright position with their stomachs facing the sun. They may then lie down and bask on their backs or spread themselves over rocks to absorb heat. During the hottest part of the day, however, they retreat to the coolness of their underground burrows or lie over damp patches of shady ground.

 SEE ALSO Dog, African Wild 2:78

Common name Dwarf mongoose

Scientific name *Helogale parvula*

Family	Herpestidae
Order	Carnivora
Size	Length head/body: 7–11 in (18–28 cm); tail length: 5.5–7.5 in (14–19 cm); height at shoulder: 5 in (12 cm)
Weight	8–13 oz (23–37 g). Male slightly smaller than female
Key features	Small, slender mongoose with short legs; coat color ranges from grayish-tan to dark brown with fine gray speckles
Habits	Active only during day; social: lives in packs of 2–20 (sometimes up to 40) individuals; searches for food as a group
Breeding	Litters of up to 6 young born after a gestation period of about 53 days. Weaned at 6–7 weeks; sexually mature at about 3 years. May live up to about 12 years in captivity, 10 in the wild
Voice	Vibrating chirrup; warning call is a shrill double note or shriek
Diet	Invertebrates, particularly crickets, grasshoppers, termites, scorpions, and spiders; vertebrate prey includes mice, lizards, snakes, and birds; some fruit
Habitat	Savannas, thickets, and woodlands, especially where there are numerous termite mounds
Distribution	Africa from Ethiopia to northern South Africa and west to northern Namibia and Angola
Status	Population: abundant. Not at risk

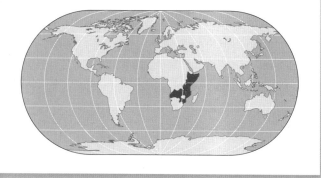

Dwarf Mongoose

Helogale parvula

The tiny dwarf mongoose resembles a short-legged cat and scurries around in groups seeking small prey. It specializes in eating the large insects and other invertebrates that are so abundant in parts of Africa.

DWARF MONGOOSES ARE THE SMALLEST members of the mongoose family. Their slender frame allows them to enter the tunnels of small rodents, which larger species are unable to do. However, their small size also means they are more vulnerable to predators than the larger species and is one reason why they live in large groups. Living in a group means there are many pairs of eyes to watch for danger, and the risk to any one mongoose is reduced by the presence of others. Like the meerkat, dwarf mongooses post guards to keep watch over the pack. The dominant male is extremely vigilant. He, along with a number of immature males, will often be seen keeping watch over the pack from a high vantage point, such as the top of a big rock or high in a bush.

Pack Hierarchy

Dwarf mongoose packs have a strict hierarchy with only one dominant breeding pair. The dominant female or "matriarch" leads the pack, and only she is able to produce young. Although other females in the pack may mate, they either do not appear to become pregnant, or their fetuses abort. If they do give birth, their young are born dead. In such cases the subordinate females still produce milk and will help suckle the matriarch's young. All pack members are involved in grooming, baby-sitting, and caring for the young when the rest of the group is out foraging. After the dominant pair, which are usually the oldest members of the pack, the youngest members are the next highest in rank. In any age group the females rank more highly than the males.

⊖ *A pair of dwarf mongooses sun themselves on a log. Dwarf mongooses are adept at protecting themselves against predators. They are known to site their dens near bee or wasp nests, which puts off potential attackers.*

 SEE ALSO Meerkat **1:**100; Mongoose, Indian Gray **1:**108; Mongoose, Banded **1:**110

Group Hunting

Dwarf mongooses also forage as a group. Because they hunt prey by chasing and pouncing and not by stalking, they do not require stealth, so the foraging success of any one individual is not hampered by the presence of others. Foraging in a group also provides protection against predators. The dwarf mongoose has developed a wide variety of calls to keep in contact with others, coordinate group movements, and warn against danger.

Dwarf mongooses have taken group feeding a step further than many other species, often forming partnerships with several species of hornbill, such as the yellow-billed, red-billed, and von der Decken's hornbills. The birds feed among the packs on insects disturbed by foraging mongooses and keep watch for predators. The birds are particularly effective at spotting attacks from the air. When they see a predator, they make warning calls and fly up into the trees. Their actions alert the mongooses to the danger so they can make their escape. The hornbills will even call when a predator is too small to be a risk to themselves. Such additional surveillance means that the dwarf mongooses can spend more time looking for food and eating rather than watching for danger. The relationship is particularly important for the mongoose guards who might not get enough food without the hornbills' presence. When there are a lot of hornbills at the food source, a dwarf mongoose pack may have none of its own members on guard at all.

Although there is some competition for food, the arrangement is mutually beneficial: If the hornbills arrive in the morning before the mongooses have emerged from their den, they call down the air vents, and the mongooses appear almost immediately. If the mongooses rise before the hornbills arrive, they will wait for the hornbills before they start foraging.

Common name Indian gray
mongoose (Indian mongoose, common Indian
mongoose, common gray mongoose,
common Bengal mongoose)

Scientific name *Herpestes edwardsii*

Family Herpestidae

Order Carnivora

Size Length head/body: 16–18 in (40–45 cm); tail
length: 16–18 in (40–45 cm); height at
shoulder: up to 8 in (20 cm)

Weight 2.2–4.5 lb (1–2 kg)

Key features Gray to light-brown coat, finely speckled
with black

Habits Solitary; agile; good climber; hunts during
the day

Breeding Litters of 2–4 young born after gestation
period of 60 days. Weaned at about 1
month; sexually mature at 2 years. May live
20 years in captivity, 8–10 in the wild

Voice Angry chatters and chirrups

Diet Small mammals, birds, and lizards; some
insects, snakes, and eggs

Habitat Open country or thin woodland

Distribution From eastern and central Arabia to Nepal,
India, and Sri Lanka. Introduced to Malaysia,
Mauritius, the West Indies, Hawaii, and the
Ryukyu and Tonaki islands of Japan

Status Population: abundant. A common animal

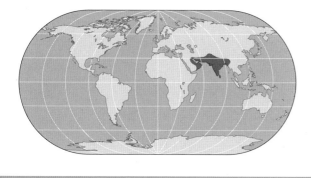

Indian Gray Mongoose

Herpestes edwardsii

*Mongooses have a reputation as snake killers that is
well deserved, but the Indian gray mongoose, like
most predators, generally prefers less dangerous prey.*

THE INDIAN GRAY MONGOOSE is an agile animal.
Although it spends most of its time on the
ground, it is also a skillful climber, able to
ascend trees and scale walls. It is active during
the day and spends the night either in an old
termite mound or in a den that it digs for itself.
Unlike some mongoose species, the Indian gray
mongoose is a solitary animal, and males and
females only form pairs for breeding. After
mating—which occurs at any time of year—the
males search for other females, leaving the
mothers to care for their young alone.

Mongoose kittens are born in a well-hidden
nest. If the mother feels her young are
threatened, she will carry them in her mouth to
another site. Newborn mongooses have a fine
covering of hair, but they are blind for several
days. The mother suckles her young for a few
weeks but then weans them onto adult food.
Once weaned, the young mongooses follow
their mother on hunting trips where she teaches
them to catch their own food. Although
mongooses are instinctive foragers and hunters,
the mother's role in passing on her hunting
skills to her young is vitally important for their
future survival. Once the young mongooses are
able to hunt for themselves, they will leave their
mother to find a territory of their own.

Stealth Tactics

Indian mongooses are more active killers than
some related species, such as the meerkat or
dwarf and banded mongooses, which mainly
forage for small invertebrate prey. The Indian
gray mongoose takes a higher proportion of
vertebrate prey, such as rats, birds, and lizards.
Hunting prey requires a high degree of skill and
stealth, and could be a reason why this species

is solitary. Traveling as a group would disturb larger prey and hence reduce hunting success. As well as vertebrate prey, the Indian gray mongoose also forages for insects by sniffing the ground and turning over rocks and stones. Fleeing prey is killed by a bite to the back of the neck or head. Mongooses are particularly fond of eggs. They break the shells by holding the egg in their front paws and throwing it between their back legs at a rock or wall.

Snake Killers

Members of the mongoose genus *Herpestes,* such as the Indian gray, are well known for their snake-killing ability. Although mongooses are not immune to snake venom, they are less sensitive to it than other mammals of a similar size. However, the main reason why mongooses do not suffer from snakebites is that they rarely receive them. In a duel between a snake and a mongoose the mongoose will avoid the snake's strikes by using a combination of speed and agility. Eventually, the snake will be worn down by the mongoose's stamina. Even constrictor species such as pythons may be overcome by the speed of a mongoose attack. However, although mongooses are capable of killing and eating snakes, they rarely feature in their diet since there are easier things to catch.

The mongooses' ability to kill dangerous snakes and their tendency to kill pest species such as mice and rats make them popular pets. Some species, including the Indian gray, have been introduced to areas around the world to help reduce snake and rat numbers. But the mongoose is an opportunist feeder, catching whatever it can find. In many areas where it has been introduced it has attacked the local fauna, often with disastrous consequences. Its fondness for eggs has also contributed to the decline of some birds, and its introduction to the Caribbean islands may have reduced the numbers of green turtles, whose eggs are laid on sandy beaches. Caribbean ground lizards, useful in keeping down insect pests, have also declined since the introduction of mongooses.

⊕ *A mongoose killing a cobra in Uttar Pradesh, India. Mongooses are renowned snake killers. The author Rudyard Kipling wrote about a duel between a mongoose named Rikki-tikki-tavi and a cobra in* **The Jungle Book.**

Common name Banded mongoose

Scientific name *Mungos mungo*

Family	Herpestidae
Order	Carnivora
Size	Length head/body: 12–18 in (30–45 cm); tail length: 6–12 in (15–30 cm); height at shoulder: 6 in (15 cm)

Weight 3–4.5 lb (1–2 kg). Male slightly heavier than female

Key features Coat usually brownish-gray, but color varies with habitat; dark-brown bands across back; feet are dark brown to black; black-tipped tail

Habits Active only during the day; social: lives in territorial packs of up to 40 members, but usually between 15 and 20; each pack has a dominant male and 3 or 4 breeding females

Breeding Up to 4 young born after gestation period of 2 months. Weaned at about 1 month; sexually mature at 10–12 months. May live up to about 12 years in captivity, 5–10 in the wild

Voice Chirps, twitters, and churrs

Diet Mainly invertebrates, particularly termites and beetle grubs in open grassland and various leaf litter invertebrates such as beetles and snails in more forested areas; some small vertebrates such as lizards, snakes, and mice; eggs and some fruit

Habitat Range of habitats from forested or cultivated areas to dry scrub and open grassland

Distribution Africa south of Sahara Desert, but not in the Congo River Basin or southwestern Africa

Status Population: abundant. Not at risk

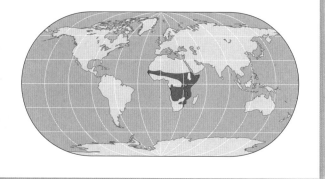

Banded Mongoose

Mungos mungo

Banded mongooses live in busy gangs that scurry around looking for small prey. They return at night to their large den, often an old termite mound.

THE BANDED MONGOOSE LIVES in large social groups—in fact, the biggest in the whole mongoose family. A pack typically has three or four breeding females and several males, rather than a single breeding pair. Banded mongoose females do not necessarily outrank males in the social hierarchy, as with dwarf mongoose females. Instead, rank appears to be based on age and individual characteristics.

Busy Foragers

Banded mongooses forage as a group led by a senior female. They busy themselves scratching up leaf litter, poking their noses and front claws into crevices, and turning over stones and dung in search of prey. Banded mongooses smash tough objects such as large millipedes and beetles, dung balls, snails, and large eggs by catapulting them between their hind legs at rocks. An individual mongoose is not inclined to share food. However, when it finds a particularly interesting food supply, a mongoose will make such excited twitters that it will soon have attracted the attention of others, who then try to grab a share.

Each group of banded mongooses uses a territory of up to 0.5 square miles (1.3 sq. km). Packs usually stay within their own territories, so meetings between packs are rare. When it does happen, it tends to be at the boundary between two territories, and both packs usually run away. Most banded mongoose dens are found in termite mounds. A den on a territory boundary may occasionally be used at different times by two different packs. If two packs turn up at the same den on the same night, the larger pack will usually chase off the others.

 SEE ALSO Meerkat **1:**100; Mongoose, Dwarf **1:**106

Mongoose packs have several dens in their territory and may use one for anything from a single night to a couple of months at a time.

The breeding cycles of females within a pack are synchronized so that all the young are born within a few days of each other. This reduces the risk to any one mongoose kitten of being caught by a predator: If births were spread out over a longer period of time, it would be easy for predators to pick off the newborn mongooses one by one. Another advantage of simultaneous births is that all the reproductive females are producing milk at the same time, and the kittens may be suckled by any female, not just their mother. Hence mothers are free to go and look for food in turn while the young are nursed by other females. Other members of the pack are also involved in caring for the young. An adult male usually remains as a baby-sitter while the rest of

⊕ Banded mongooses find refuge in a termite mound. It may be one of a number of dens scattered over the pack's territory and used when the need arises.

the group is out foraging. The young leave the den at three to four weeks old and join the rest of the pack in play. Once they are about five weeks old, the kittens will begin to accompany the adults on foraging expeditions.

Safety in Numbers

Unlike the smaller dwarf mongoose—whose only response to potential predators is to run for cover—banded mongooses may club together and take part in mobbing attacks. During such attacks all members of the pack bunch closely together and advance with their heads raised. The resulting growling and snapping mass can give the impression of a single large animal. The displays can be so impressive that they intimidate large dogs and other predators such as jackals, eagles, and vultures. But banded mongooses may also mob harmless animals, such as bushbucks and geese, if they seem to pose a threat. When a pack is on the defensive, it bunches up with the young in the center. Protection of fellow group members may even extend to rescuing captured individuals. For example, when a banded mongoose was caught by an eagle and taken into a tree to be eaten, a dominant male from the pack was observed to climb the tree and force the eagle to release its catch.

List of Species

The following lists all species of small carnivores, including their distribution:

Order Carnivora (Part)

FAMILY PROCYONIDAE
Raccoon Family

SUBFAMILY PROCYONINAE
Bassariscus
B. astutus Ringtail (civet, miner's, or ringtailed cat); W. U.S. from Oregon and Colorado south and throughout Mexico
B. sumichrasti Cacomistle; C. America

Nasua
N. narica White-nosed coati; S.E. Arizona, Mexico, C. America, W. Colombia, and Ecuador
N. nasua Ringtailed coati; S. America east of Andes south to N. Argentina and Uruguay

Nasuella
N. olivacea Mountain coati; Ecuador, W. Venezuela, and Colombia

Procyon
P. cancrivorus Crab-eating raccoon; Costa Rica to N. Argentina
P. gloverallmi Barbados raccoon; Barbados
P. insularis Tres Marías raccoon; María Madre Island, Mexico
P. lotor Common raccoon; S. Canada, U.S., C. America; introduced in parts of Europe and Asia
P. maynardi Nassau Island, Bahamas
P. minor Guadeloupe raccoon; Guadeloupe
P. pygmaeus Cozumel Island raccoon; Cozumel Island, Yucatán, Mexico

SUBFAMILY POTOSINAE
Bassaricyon Olingos
B. alleni Amazonia
B. beddardi Guyana
B. gabbi C. America and N.W. South America
B. lasius Costa Rica
B. pauli Panama

Potos
P. flavus Kinkajou; E. Central and S. America from S. Mexico to Brazil

SUBFAMILY AILURINAE
Ailurus
C. fulgens Red panda; Himalayas to S. China

FAMILY MUSTELIDAE
Weasel Family

SUBFAMILY MUSTELINAE
Eira
E. barbara Tayra; C. and S. America; Trinidad

Galictis
G. cuja Little grison; C. and S. America
G. vittata Grison (huron); C. and S. America from Mexico to Brazil

Gulo
G. gulo Wolverine; circumpolar, in N. America and Eurasia

Ictonyx
I. striatus Zorilla (African or striped polecat); semiarid regions of Africa south of Sahara

Lyncodon
L. patagonicus Patagonian weasel; pampas of Argentina and Chile

Martes
M. americana American marten; northern N. America to Sierra Nevada and Rockies in Colorado and California
M. flavigula Yellow-throated marten; S.E. Asia to Korea, Java, Sumatra, and Borneo
M. foina Stone marten (beech or house marten); S. and C. Europe to Denmark and C. Asia
M. gwatkinsi Nilgiri marten (yellow-throated marten); Nilgiri Mountains of S. India
M. martes Pine marten; C. and N. Europe, W. Asia
M. melampus Japanese marten; Japan, Korea
M. pennanti Fisher (Pekan or Virginian polecat); northern N. America to California (Sierra Nevada) and W. Virginia (Appalachians)
M. zibellina Sable; N. Asia, N. Japanese islands

Mustela
M. africana Tropical weasel; E. Peru, Brazil
M. altaica Mountain weasel; forested mountains of Asia from Altai to Korea and Tibet
M. erminea Stoat (ermine or short-tailed weasel); N. America and Eurasia south to about 40°N, including Ireland and Japan, but not semideserts of Kazakhstan and Mongolia, Mediterranean region, or N. Africa; introduced to New Zealand
M. eversmannii Steppe polecat; steppes and semideserts of Russia, Kazakhstan, and Mongolia to China
M. felipei Colombian weasel; highlands of Colombia
M. frenata Long-tailed weasel; N. America from about 50° north to Panama extending through northern S. America along Andes to Bolivia
M. kathiah Yellow-bellied weasel; Himalayas, W. and S. China, N. Myanmar
M. lutreola European mink; confined to a few declining populations in E. Europe and Spain
M. lutreolina Indonesian mountain weasel; high altitudes of Java and Sumatra
M. nigripes Black-footed ferret; western prairies of N. America; was rated extinct in the wild, but maintained in captivity and being locally reintroduced

M. nivalis Least weasel (European common weasel); N. America from Arctic to about 40°; Europe from Atlantic seaboard (except Ireland), including Azores, Mediterranean islands; N. Africa and Egypt east across Asia north of Himalayas; introduced in New Zealand
M. nudipes Barefoot weasel; S.E. Asia, Sumatra, Borneo
M. putorius European polecat; Europe except most of Scandinavia to Urals
M. sibirica Kolinsky; European Russia to E. Siberia, Korea, China, Japan, and Taiwan
M. strigidorsa Back-striped weasel; Nepal east through N. Myanmar to Indochina
M. vison American mink (eastern mink); originally N. America, but now naturalized throughout Europe, C. and E. Asia, and southern S. America

Poecilictis
P. libyca North African banded weasel; semidesert fringes of the Sahara from Morocco and Egypt to N. Nigeria and Sudan

Poecilogale
P. albinucha African striped weasel; Africa south of Sahara

Vormela
V. peregusna Marbled polecat; steppe and semidesert from S.E. Europe (Romania) east to W. China, Palestine, Baluchistan

SUBFAMILY LUTRINAE
Amblonyx
A. cinereus Short-clawed otter; India, Sri Lanka, S.E. Asia, Indonesia, Borneo, Palawan Islands, S. China

Aonyx
A. capensis Cape clawless otter; Africa south of 15°N from Senegal to Ethiopia south to the Cape; absent only from desert regions of Namibia
A. congicus Congo clawless otter; African forest; streams and rivers of the Congo Basin

Enhydra
E. lutris Sea otter; Kurile and Aleutian Islands, Alaskan coast, Gulf of Alaska; reintroduced into parts of former range along Pacific coast of N. America (notably California) and Russia

Lontra
L. canadensis North American river otter (Canadian otter); Canada, U.S. including Alaska
L. felina Marine otter; coast and coastal islands of Chile and Peru
L. longicaudis Neotropical river otter; C. and S. America from Mexico to Argentina
L. provocax Southern river otter; Argentina, Chile

Lutra
L. lutra European river otter (Eurasian river otter); Eurasia south of tundra line, N. Africa
L. maculicollis Spot-necked otter; Africa south of Sahara; absent from desert areas like Namibia

L. sumatrana Hairy-nosed otter; Sumatra, Java, Borneo, Thailand, Vietnam, Malaysia

Lutrogale
L. perspicillata Smooth-coated otter; Iraq (Tigris River), lower Indus, India, S.E. Asia, Myanmar, S.W. China, Malay Peninsula, Sumatra, Borneo

Pteronura
P. brasiliensis Giant otter; in all countries of S. America except possibly Chile, Argentina, and Uruguay

SUBFAMILY MELINAE
Arctonyx
A. collaris Hog badger; Peking in north throughout S. China and Indochina to Thailand, and Sumatra

Meles
M. meles European badger (Eurasian badger); N. Europe up to S. Scandinavia, European Russia up to Arctic Circle south to Palestine east to Iran, Tibet, and S. China

Melogale Ferret badgers
M. everetti Everett's ferret badger; Borneo
M. moschata Chinese ferret badger; China, Taiwan, Assam, Myanmar, and S.E. Asia
M. orientalis Oriental ferret badger; Java, Bali, and S.E. Asia
M. personata Indian ferret badger; India, Nepal, Myanmar

Mydaus
M. javanensis Teledu (Malaysian or Indonesian stink badger); Borneo, Sumatra, Java, and N. Natuna Islands
M. marchei Palawan stink badger; Palawan and Busuanga N.E. of Borneo

SUBFAMILY ELLIVORINAE
Mellivora
M. capensis Honey badger; Africa from Cape to Morocco in west and Ethiopia, Sudan, and Somalia in east; Arabia to Turkmenistan, Nepal, and India

SUBFAMILY TAXIDIINAE
Taxidea
T. taxus American badger; from S.W. Canada and N.C. U.S. south to Mexico

SUBFAMILY MEPHITINAE
Conepatus Hog-nosed skunks
C. chinga Andes skunk; Argentina, Bolivia, Chile, Paraguay, Peru
C. humboldtii Patagonian skunk; S. Chile, Argentina
C. leuconotus Eastern hog-nosed skunk; E. Texas, E. Mexico
C. mesoleucus Western hog-nosed skunk; S. U.S., Nicaragua
C. semistriatus Amazonian skunk; S. Mexico, N. Peru, E. Brazil

Mephitis
M. macroura Hooded skunk; S.W. U.S.
M. mephitis Striped skunk; S. Canada, U.S., N. Mexico

Spilogale Spotted skunks
S. gracilis Western spotted skunk; W. U.S. to C. Mexico
S. putorius Eastern spotted skunk; S.E. and C. U.S. to E. Mexico
S. pygmaea Pygmy skunk; W. and S.W. Mexico

FAMILY VIVERRIDAE
Civet and Genet Family

SUBFAMILY NANDINIIAE
Nandinia
N. binotata African palm civet (two-spotted palm civet); from Guinea (including Fernando Póo Island) to S. Sudan in the north, to Mozambique, E. Zimbabwe, and C. Angola in south

SUBFAMILY PARADOXURINAE
Arctictus
A. binturong Binturong (bear cat); India, Nepal, Bhutan, Myanmar, Thailand, Malaysia, Indochina, Sumatra, Java, Borneo, Palawan
Arctogalidia
A. trivirgata Small-toothed palm civet (three-striped palm civet); Assam, Myanmar, Thailand, Malayan and Indochinese peninsulas, China (Yunnan), Sumatra, Java, Borneo, Riau-Lingga Archipelago, Bangka, Bilitung, N. Natuna Islands
Macrogalidia
M. musschenbroekii Sulawesi palm civet (giant civet or brown palm civet); N.E. and C. Sulawesi (Celebes)
Paguma
P. larvata Masked palm civet; India, Nepal, Tibet, China north to Hopei, Shansi, Taiwan, Hainan, Myanmar, Thailand, Malaya, Sumatra, N. Borneo, S. Andaman Islands; introduced to Japan
Paradoxurus
P. hermaphroditus Common palm civet (toddy cat); India, Sri Lanka, Nepal, Assam, Bhutan, Myanmar, Thailand, S. China, Malaya, Indochina, Sumatra, Java, Borneo, Ceram, Kei Islands, Nusa Tenggara (Lesser Sunda Islands) as far east as Timor, Philippines
P. jerdoni Jerdon's palm civet; S. India (Palni and Nilgiri Hills, Travancore, and Coorg)
P. zeylonensis Golden palm civet; Sri Lanka

SUBFAMILY HEMIGALINAE
Chrotogale
C. owstoni Owston's banded civet (Owston's palm civet); north of Indochinese peninsula
Cynogale
C. bennettii Otter civet (water civet); Sumatra, Borneo, Malayan and Indochinese Peninsulas
C. lowei Lowe's otter civet; N. Vietnam
Diplogale
D. hosei Hose's palm civet; Borneo, Sarawak—Mount Dulit to 3,900 ft (1,200 m)
Hemigalus
H. derbyanus Banded palm civet;

Peninsular Myanmar, Malaya, Sumatra, Borneo, Sipora and S. Pagai Islands

SUBFAMILY VIVERRINAE
Civettictis
C. civetta African civet; Senegal east to Somalia in north through C. and E. Africa to KwaZulu-Natal, Transvaal, N. Botswana, and N. Namibia in south
Genetta
G. abyssinica Abyssinian genet; Ethiopian highlands, Somalia
G. angolensis Angolan genet (Mozambique genet, Hinton's genet); N. Angola, Mozambique, S. Democratic Republic of Congo, N.W. Zambia, S. Tanzania
G. felina Feline genet; Africa south of the Sahara except for rain forest; S. Arabian Peninsula
G. genetta Common genet (small-spotted genet or European genet); Africa (north of Sahara), Iberian Peninsula, France, Palestine
G. johnstoni Johnston's genet (Lehmann's genet); Liberia
G. maculata (formerly *G. pardina*) Forest genet; southern part of W. Africa, C. Africa, S. Africa (except Cape region)
G. servalina Servaline genet (small-spotted genet); C. Africa, with restricted range in E. Africa
G. thierryi Villier's genet (false genet); W. Africa
G. tigrina Large-spotted genet (blotched genet or tigrine genet); Cape region of S. Africa
G. victoriae Giant genet (giant forest genet); Uganda, N. DRC
Poiana
P. richardsoni African linsang (oyan); Sierra Leone, Côte d'Ivoire, Gabon, Cameroon, N. Congo, Fernando Póo Island
Prionodon
P. linsang Banded linsang; W. Malaysia, Tenasserim, Sumatra, Java, Borneo
P. pardicolor Spotted linsang; Nepal, Assam, Sikkim, N. Myanmar, Indochina
Osbornictis
O. piscivora Aquatic genet (fishing genet or Congo water civet); Kisangani and Kibale-Ituri districts of DRC
Viverra
V. megaspila Large-spotted civet; S. Myanmar, Thailand, formerly the coastal district and W. Ghats of S. India; Indochina, Malay Peninsula to Penang
V. tangalunga Malayan civet (Oriental or ground civet, tangalunga); Malaya, Sumatra, Riau-Lingga Archipelago, Borneo, Sulawesi, Karlinata, Bangka, Buru, Ambon and Langkawi Islands, Philippines
V. zibetha Large Indian civet; N. India, Nepal, Myanmar, Thailand, Indochina, Malaya, S. China
Viverricula
V. indica Small Indian civet (rasse);

S. China, Myanmar, W. Malaysia, Thailand, Sumatra, Java, Bali, Hainan, Taiwan, Indochina, India, Sri Lanka, Bhutan; introduced to Madagascar, Sokotra, and Comoro Islands

SUBFAMILY EUPLERINAE
Eupleres
E. goudotii Falanouc; E.C. to N.W. Madagascar
Fossa
F. fossa Fanaloka (Madagascar or Malagasy civet); Madagascar

SUBFAMILY CRYPTOPROCTINAE
Cryptoprocta
C. ferox Fossa; Madagascar

FAMILY HERPESTIDAE
Mongoose Family

SUBFAMILY HERPESTINAE
Atilax
A. paludinosus Marsh mongoose (water mongoose); Gambia east to Ethiopia south to S. Africa
Bdeogale
B. crassicauda Bushy-tailed mongoose; Mozambique, Malawi, Zambia, Tanzania, Kenya
B. jacksoni Jackson's mongoose; C. Kenya and S.E. Uganda
B. nigripes Black-legged mongoose; Nigeria to N. Angola, C. Kenya, S.E. Uganda
Crossarchus
C. alexandri Alexander's mongoose (Congo mongoose); DRC, W. Uganda, Mount Elgon, Kenya
C. ansorgei Angolan mongoose; N. Angola, S.E. DRC
C. obscurus Kusimanse (dark mongoose, long-nosed mongoose); Sierra Leone, Cameroon
Cynictis
C. penicillata Yellow mongoose (red meerkat); S. Africa, Namibia, S. Angola, Botswana
Dologale
D. dybowskii Pousargue's mongoose (Dybowski's or African tropical savanna mongoose); N.E. DRC, C. African Republic, S. Sudan, W. Uganda
Helogale
H. parvula Dwarf mongoose; Ethiopia to northern S. Africa west to N. Namibia
Herpestes
H. brachyurus Short-tailed mongoose; Malaysia, Sumatra, Java, Philippines
H. edwardsii Indian gray mongoose; E. and C. Arabia to Nepal, India, and Sri Lanka
H. (Galerella) flavescens N. and C. Namibia, S. Angola
H. fuscus Indian brown mongoose; S. India, Sri Lanka
H. ichneumon Egyptian mongoose (Ichneumon); most of Africa except Sahara, C. and W. African forest regions, and S.W. Africa; Israel, S. Spain, and Portugal
H. javanicus (includes *H. auropunctatus*) Small Indian mongoose (Javan gold-spotted

mongoose); N. Arabia to S. China and Malay Peninsula; Sumatra, Java; introduced to W. Indies, Hawaiian Islands, Fiji
H. naso Long-nosed mongoose; S.E. Nigeria to Gabon and DRC
H. (Galerella) pulverulentus Cape gray mongoose; S. Angola, Namibia, S. Africa
H. (Galerella) sanguineus Slender mongoose; Africa south of Sahara
H. smithii Ruddy mongoose; India, Sri Lanka
H. (Galerella) swalius; S. and C. Namibia
H. urva Crab-eating mongoose; S. China, Nepal, Assam, Myanmar, Indochinese peninsula, Taiwan, Hainan, Sumatra, Borneo, Philippines
H. vitticollis Stripe-necked mongoose; S. India, Sri Lanka
Ichneumia
I. albicauda White-tailed mongoose; Sub-Saharan Africa except C. and W. African forest regions and S.W. Africa; S. Arabia
Liberiictis
L. kuhni Liberian mongoose; Liberia
Mungos
M. gambianus Gambian mongoose; Gambia to Nigeria
M. mungo Banded mongoose; Africa south of Sahara, except Congo and S.W. Africa
Paracynictis
P. selousi Selous's mongoose (gray meerkat); southern Africa from Angola to northern S. Africa
Rhynchogale
R. melleri Meller's mongoose; S. DRC, Tanzania, Malawi, Zambia, C. and N. Mozambique
Suricata
S. suricatta Suricate (meerkat, gray meerkat, or stoksterje); Angola, Namibia, S. Africa, S. Botswana

SUBFAMILY GALIDIINAE
Galidia
G. elegans Ringtailed mongoose; Madagascar
Galidictis
G. fasciata Broad-striped mongoose (Madagascar banded mongoose); Madagascar
G. grandidieri Giant striped mongoose; desert of S.W. Madagascar
Mungotictis
M. decemlineata Narrow-striped mongoose; W. Madagascar
Salanoia
S. concolor Brown mongoose; E. Madagascar

Glossary

Words in SMALL CAPITALS refer to other entries in the glossary.

Adaptation features of an animal that adjust it to its environment; may be produced by evolution—e.g., camouflage coloration

Adaptive radiation when a group of closely related animals (e.g., members of a FAMILY) have evolved differences from each other so that they can survive in different NICHES

Adult a fully grown animal that has reached breeding age

Amphibian any cold-blooded VERTEBRATE of the class Amphibia, typically living on land but breeding in the water, e.g., frogs, toads, and newts

Anal gland (anal sac) a gland opening by a short duct either just inside the anus or on either side of it

Aquatic living in water

Arboreal living among the branches of trees

Arthropod animals with a jointed outer skeleton, e.g., crabs and insects

Biodiversity a variety of SPECIES and the variation within them

Biomass the total weight of living material

Biped any animal that walks on two legs. See QUADRUPED

Breeding season the entire cycle of reproductive activity from courtship, pair formation (and often establishment of TERRITORY), through nesting to independence of young

Browsing feeding on leaves of trees and shrubs

Cache a hidden supply of food; also (verb) to hide food for future use

Callosities hardened, thickened areas on the skin (e.g., ischial callosities in some PRIMATES)

Canine (tooth) a sharp stabbing tooth usually longer than rest

Canopy continuous (closed) or broken (open) layer in forests produced by the intermingling of branches of trees

Capillaries tiny blood vessels that convey blood through organs from arteries to veins

Carnassial (teeth) opposing pair of teeth especially adapted to shear with a cutting (scissorlike) edge; in living mammals the arrangement is unique to Carnivora, and the teeth involved are the fourth upper PREMOLAR and first lower MOLAR

Carnivore meat-eating animal

Carrion dead animal matter used as a food source by scavengers

Cecum a blind sac in the digestive tract opening out from the junction between the small and large intestines. In herbivorous mammals it is often very large; it is the site of bacterial action on CELLULOSE. The end of the cecum is the appendix; in SPECIES with a reduced cecum the appendix may retain an antibacterial function

Cellulose the material that forms the cell walls of plants

Cementum hard material that coats the roots of mammalian teeth. In some SPECIES cementum is laid down in annual layers that, under a microscope, can be counted to estimate the age of individuals

Cheek pouch a pocket in or alongside the mouth used for the temporary storage of food

Cheek teeth teeth lying behind the CANINES, consisting of PREMOLARS and MOLARS

CITES Convention on International Trade in Endangered Species. An agreement between nations that restricts international trade to permitted levels through a system of licensing and administrative controls. Rare animals and plants are assigned to categories: (for instance Appendix 1, 2). See Volume 1 page 17

Cloven hoof foot that is formed from two toes, each within a horny covering

Congenital condition animal is born with

Coniferous forest evergreen forests of northern regions and mountainous areas dominated by pines, spruces, and cedars

Corm underground food storage bulb of certain plants

Crepuscular active in twilight

Cursorial adapted for running

Deciduous forest dominated by trees that lose their leaves in winter (or the dry season)

Deforestation the process of cutting down and removing trees for timber or to create open space for activities such as growing crops or grazing animals

Delayed implantation when the development of a fertilized egg is suspended for a variable period before it implants into the wall of the UTERUS and completes normal pregnancy. Births are thus delayed until a favorable time of year

Den a shelter, natural or constructed, used for sleeping, giving birth, and raising young; also (verb) the act of retiring to a den to give birth and raise young, or for winter shelter

Dental formula convention for summarizing the dental arrangement, in which the numbers of all types of tooth in each half of the upper and lower jaw are given. The numbers are always presented in the order: INCISOR (I), CANINE (C), PREMOLAR (P), MOLAR (M). The final figure is the total number of teeth to be found in the skull. A typical example for Carnivora is I3/3, C1/1, P4/4, M3/3 = 44

Dentition animal's set of teeth

Desert area of low rainfall dominated by specially adapted plants such as cacti

Digit a finger or toe

Digitigrade method of walking on the toes without the heel touching the ground. See PLANTIGRADE

Dispersal the scattering of young animals going to live away from where they were born and brought up

Display any relatively conspicuous pattern of behavior that conveys specific information to others, usually to members of the same SPECIES; can involve visual or vocal elements, as in threat, courtship, or greeting displays

Diurnal active during the day

DNA (deoxyribonucleic acid) the substance that makes up the main part of the chromosomes of all living things; contains the genetic code that is handed down from generation to generation

DNA analysis "genetic fingerprinting," a technique that allows scientists to see who is related to whom, for example, which male was the father of particular offspring

Domestication process of taming and breeding animals to provide help and useful products for humans

Dorsal relating to the back or spinal part of the body; usually the upper surface

Droppings see FECES and SCATS

Ecosystem a whole system in which plants, animals, and their environment interact

Edentate toothless, but is also used as group name for anteaters, sloths, and armadillos

Endemic found only in one small geographical area, nowhere else

Estivation inactivity or greatly decreased activity during hot or dry weather

Estrus the period when eggs are released from the female's ovaries, and she becomes available for successful mating. Estrous females are often referred to as "in heat" or as "RECEPTIVE" to males

Eutherian mammals that give birth to babies, not eggs, and rear them without using a pouch on the mother's belly

Extinction the process of dying out in which every last individual dies, and the SPECIES is lost forever

Eyeshine when eyes of animals (especially CARNIVORES) reflect a beam of light shone at them. It is caused by a special reflective layer (the tapetum) at the back of the eye characteristic of many NOCTURNAL species and associated with an increased ability to see in the dark

Family technical term for group of closely related SPECIES that often also look quite similar. Zoological family names always end in "idae." See Volume 1 page 11. Also, a social group within a species consisting of parents and their offspring

Feces remains of digested food expelled from body as pellets, often with SCENT secretions

Feral domestic animals that have gone wild and live independently of people

Flystrike where CARRION-feeding flies have laid their eggs

Fossorial adapted for digging and living in burrows or underground tunnels

Frugivore an animal that eats fruit as main part of the diet

Fur mass of hairs forming a continuous coat characteristic of mammals

Fused joined together

Gape wide-open mouth

Gene the basic unit of heredity enabling one generation to pass on characteristics to its offspring

Generalist an animal that is capable of a wide range of activities, not specialized

Genus a group of closely related SPECIES. The plural is genera. See Volume 1 page 11

Gestation the period of pregnancy between fertilization of the egg and birth of the baby

Grazing feeding on grass

Gregarious living together in loose groups or herds

Harem a group of females living in the same TERRITORY and consorting with a single male

Herbivore an animal that eats plants (grazers and browsers are thus herbivores)

Heterodont DENTITION specialized into CANINES, INCISORS, and PREMOLARS, each type of tooth having a different function. See HOMODONT

Hibernation becoming inactive in winter, with lowered body temperature to save energy. Hibernation takes place in a special nest or DEN called a hibernaculum

Homeothermy maintenance of a high and constant body temperature by means of internal processes; also called "warm-blooded"

Home range the area that an animal uses in the course of its normal periods of activity. See TERRITORY

Homodont DENTITION in which the teeth are all similar in appearance and function

Horns a pair of sharp, unbranched prongs projecting from the head of CLOVEN-HOOFED animals. Horns have a bony core with a tough outer covering made of KERATIN like fingernails

Hybrid offspring of two closely related SPECIES that can interbreed, but the hybrid is sterile

Inbreeding breeding among closely related animals (e.g., cousins) leading to weakened genetic composition and reduced survival rates

Incisor (teeth) simple pointed teeth at the front of the jaws used for nipping and snipping

Indigenous living naturally in a region; NATIVE (i.e., not an introduced SPECIES)

Insectivore animals that feed on insects and similar small prey. Also used as a group name for animals such as hedgehogs, shrews, and moles

Interbreeding breeding between animals of different SPECIES or varieties within a single FAMILY or strain; interbreeding can cause dilution of the gene pool

Interspecific between SPECIES

Intraspecific between individuals of the same SPECIES

Invertebrates animals that have no backbone (or other true bones) inside their body, e.g., mollusks, insects, jellyfish, and crabs

IUCN International Union for the Conservation of Nature, responsible for assigning animals and plants to internationally agreed categories of rarity. See table below

Juvenile young animal that has not yet reached breeding age

Kelp brown seaweeds

Keratin tough, fibrous material that forms hairs, feathers, and protective plates on the skin of VERTEBRATE animals

Lactation process of producing milk in MAMMARY GLANDS for offspring

Larynx voice box where sounds are created

Latrine place where FECES are left regularly, often with SCENT added

Leptospirosis disease caused by leptospiral bacteria in kidneys and transmitted via urine

Mammary glands characteristic of mammals, glands for production of milk

Marine living in the sea

Matriarch senior female member of a social group

Metabolic rate the rate at which chemical activities occur within animals, including the exchange of gasses in respiration and the liberation of energy from food

Metabolism the chemical activities within animals that turn food into energy

Migration movement from one place to another and back again, usually seasonal

Molars large crushing teeth at the back of the mouth

Molt process in which mammals shed hair, usually seasonal

Monogamous animals that have only one mate at a time

Montane in a mountain environment

Musk mammalian SCENT

Mutation random changes in genetic material

Native belonging to that area or country, not introduced by human assistance

IUCN CATEGORIES

EX Extinct, when there is no reasonable doubt that the last individual of a species has died.

EW Extinct in the Wild, when a species is known only to survive in captivity or as a naturalized population well outside the past range.

CR Critically Endangered, when a species is facing an extremely high risk of extinction in the wild in the immediate future.

EN Endangered, when a species faces a very high risk of extinction in the wild in the near future.

VU Vulnerable, when a species faces a high risk of extinction in the wild in the medium-term future.

LR Lower Risk, when a species has been evaluated and does not satisfy the criteria for CR, EN, or VU.

DD Data Deficient, when there is not enough information about a species to assess the risk of extinction.

NE Not Evaluated, species that have not been assessed by the IUCN criteria.

Natural selection when animals and plants are challenged by natural processes (including predation and bad weather) to ensure survival of the fittest

New World the Americas; OLD WORLD refers to the non-American continents (not usually Australia)

Niche part of a habitat occupied by an ORGANISM, defined in terms of all aspects of its lifestyle

Nocturnal active at night

Nomadic animals that have no fixed home, but wander continuously

Old World non-American continents. See NEW WORLD

Olfaction sense of smell

Omnivore an animal that eats almost anything, meat or vegetable

Opportunistic taking advantage of every varied opportunity that arises, flexible behavior

Opposable fingers or toes that can be brought to bear against others on the same hand or foot in order to grip objects

Order a subdivision of a class of animals consisting of a series of related animal FAMILIES. See Volume 1 page 11

Ovulation release of egg from the female's ovary prior to its fertilization

Pair bond behavior that keeps a male and a female together beyond the time it takes to mate; marriage is a "pair bond"

Parasite animal or plant that lives on or in body of another

Parturition process of giving birth

Pelage the furry coat of a mammal

Pelt furry coat; often refers to skin removed from animal as fur

Pheromone SCENT produced by animals to enable others to find and recognize them

Physiology the processes and workings within plants and animal bodies, e.g., digestion. Keeping a warm-blooded state is a part of mammal physiology

Placenta the structure that links an embryo to its mother during pregnancy, allowing exchange of chemicals between them

Plantigrade walking on the soles of the feet with the heels touching the ground. See DIGITIGRADE

Polygamous when animals have more than one mate in a single mating season. MONOGOMOUS animals have only a single mate

Polygynous when a male mates with several females in one BREEDING SEASON

Population a distinct group of animals of the same SPECIES or all the animals of that species

Posterior the hind end or behind another structure

Predator an animal that kills live prey for food

Prehensile grasping tail or fingers

Premolars teeth found in front of MOLARS, but behind CANINES

Pride social group of lions

Primate a group of mammals that includes monkeys, apes, and ourselves

Promiscuous mating often with many mates, not just one

Protein chemicals made up of amino acids. Essential in the diet of animals

Quadruped an animal that walks on all fours (a BIPED walks on two legs)

Range the total geographical area over which a SPECIES is distributed

Receptive when a female is ready to mate (in ESTRUS)

Reproduction the process of breeding, creating new offspring for the next generation

Retina light-sensitive layer at the back of the eye. May include a tapetum, a reflective layer causing EYESHINE when a beam of light is shone at the eyes

Retractile capable of being withdrawn, as in the claws of typical cats, which can be folded back into the paws to protect from damage when walking

Riparian living beside rivers and lakes

Roadkill animals killed by road traffic

Rumen complex stomach found in RUMINANTS specifically for digesting plant material

Ruminant animals that eat vegetation and later bring it back from the stomach to chew again ("chewing the cud" or "rumination") to assist its digestion by microbes in the stomach

Savanna tropical grasslands with scattered trees and low rainfall, usually in warm areas

Scats fecal pellets, especially of CARNIVORES. SCENT is often deposited with the pellets as territorial markers

Scent chemicals produced by animals to leave smell messages for others to find and interpret

Scrotum bag of skin within which the male testicles are located

Scrub vegetation that is dominated by shrubs—woody plants usually with more than one stem

Secondary forest trees that have been planted or grown up on cleared ground

Siblings brothers and sisters

Social behavior interactions between individuals within the same SPECIES, e.g., courtship

Species a group of animals that look similar and can breed to produce fertile offspring

Spraint hunting term for SCATS (see above) of certain CARNIVORES, especially otters

Steppe open grassland in parts of the world where the climate is too harsh for trees to grow

Sub-Saharan all parts of Africa lying south of the Sahara Desert

Subspecies a locally distinct group of animals that differ slightly from the normal appearance of the SPECIES; often called a race

Symbiosis when two or more SPECIES live together for their mutual benefit more successfully than either could live on its own

Taxonomy the branch of biology concerned with classifying ORGANISMS into groups according to similarities in their structure, origins, or behavior. The categories, in order of increasing broadness, are: SPECIES, GENUS, FAMILY, ORDER, class, and phylum. See Volume 1 page 11

Terrestrial living on land

Territory defended space

Thermoregulation the maintenance of a relatively constant body temperature either by adjustments to METABOLISM or by moving between sunshine and shade

Torpor deep sleep accompanied by lowered body temperature and reduced METABOLIC RATE

Translocation transferring members of a SPECIES from one location to another

Tundra open grassy or shrub-covered lands of the far north

Underfur fine hairs forming a dense, woolly mass close to the skin and underneath the outer coat of stiff hairs in mammals

Ungulate hoofed animals such as pigs, deer, cattle, and horses; mostly HERBIVORES

Uterus womb in which embryos of mammals develop

Ventral the belly or underneath of an animal (opposite of DORSAL)

Vertebrate animal with a backbone (e.g., fish, mammals, reptiles), usually with a skeleton made of bones, but sometimes softer cartilage

Vibrissae sensory whiskers, usually on snout, but can be on areas such as elbows, tail, or eyebrows

Viviparous animals that give birth to active young rather than laying eggs

Vocalization making of sounds such as barking and croaking

Zoologist person who studies animals

Zoology the study of animals

Further Reading

General

Cranbrook, G., **The Mammals of Southeast Asia**, Oxford University Press, New York, NY, 1991

Eisenberg, J. F., and Redford, K. H., **The Mammals of the Neotropics,** University of Chicago Press, Chicago, IL, 1999

Estes, R. D., **The Behavioral Guide to African Mammals**, University of California Press, Berkley, CA, 1991

Garbutt, N., **The Mammals of Madagascar**, Pica Press, Sussex, U.K., 1999

Harrison, D. L., and Bates, P. P. J. J., **The Mammals of Arabia**, Sevenoaks, U.K., 1991

King, C. M., **The Handbook of New Zealand Mammals**, Oxford University Press, Oxford, U.K., 1995

Kingdon, J., **The Kingdon Field Guide to African Mammals**, Academic Press, San Diego, CA, 1997

MacDonald, D., **Collins Field Guide to the Mammals of Britain and Europe**, Harper Collins, New York, NY, 1993

MacDonald, D., **The Encyclopedia of Mammals**, Barnes and Noble, New York, NY, 2001

Nowak, R. M., **Walker's Mammals of the World**, The John Hopkins University Press, Baltimore, MD, 1999

Skinner, J. D., and Smithers, R. H. N., **The Mammals of the Southern African Subregion**, University of Pretoria, Pretoria, South Africa, 1990

Strahan, R., **The Mammals of Australia**, Reed New Holland, Australia, 1998

Whitaker, J. O., **National Audubon Society Field Guide to North American Mammals**, Alfred A. Knopf, New York, NY, 1996

Wilson, D. E., **The Smithsonian Book of North American Mammals**, Smithsonian Institution Press, Washington, DC, 1999

Wilson, D. E., and Reeder, D.M., **Mammal Species of the World. A Taxonomic and Geographical Reference**. Smithsonian Institution Press, Washington, DC, 1999

Young, J. Z., **The Life of Mammals: Their Anatomy and Physiology**, Oxford University Press, Oxford, U.K., 1975

Specific to this volume

Buskirk, S. W., Martens, **Sables, and Fishers: Biology and Conservation**, Cornell University Press, Ithaca, NY, 1994

Dennis, N., and Macdonald, M., **Meerkats**, Struik, South Africa, 1999

Gittelman, J. L., **Carnivore Behavior, Ecology, and Evolution**, Cornell University Press, Ithaca, NY, 1996

Griffiths, H. I., **Mustelids in a Modern World**, Backhuys, Leiden, Netherlands, 2000

Jackson, P., **Weasels, Badgers, Civets and Mongooses, and their Relatives**, IUCN, Switzerland and Cambridge, U.K., 1990

MacDonald, D., **The Velvet Claw, B.B.C Books**, London, U.K.,1992

Neal, E., and Cheeseman, C., **Badgers**, Poyser, London, U.K.,1995

Useful Websites

General

http://animaldiversity.ummz.umich.edu/
University of Michigan Museum of Zoology animal diversity websites. Search for pictures and information about animals by class, family, and common name. Includes glossary

http://www.cites.org/
IUCN and CITES listings. Search for animals by scientific name, order, family, genus, species, or common name. Location by country and explanation of reasons for listings

http://endangered.fws.gov
Information about threatened animals and plants from the U.S. Fish and Wildlife Service, the organization in charge of 94 million acres (38 million ha) of American wildlife refuges

http://www.iucn.org
Details of species and their status; listings by the International Union for the Conservation of Nature, also lists IUCN publications

http://www.panda.org
World Wide Fund for Nature (WWF), newsroom, press releases, government reports, campaigns

http://www.aza.org
American Zoo and Aquarium Association

http://www.ultimateungulate.com
Guide to world's hoofed mammals

http://www.wcs.org
Website of the Wildlife Conservation Society

http://www.nwf.org
Website of the National Wildlife Federation

http://www.nmnh.si.edu/msw/
Mammals list on Smithsonian Museum site

Specific to this volume

http://www.carnivoreconservation.org/
News, links, recent books, etc., on carnivore ecology and conservation

http://www.defenders.org/
Active conservation of carnivores, including wolves and grizzly bears

http://www.wwfcanada.org/en/res_links/pdf/projdesc.pdf
Carnivore conservation in the Rocky Mountains

http://www.5tigers.org
Comprehensive information about tigers

117

Set Index

A **bold** number shows the volume and is followed by the relevant page numbers (e.g., **1**: 52, 74).

Common names in **bold** (e.g., **aardwolf**) mean that the animal has an illustrated main entry in the set. Underlined page numbers (e.g., **9**: 78–79) refer to the main entry for that animal.

Italic page numbers (e.g., **2**: *103*) point to illustrations of animals in parts of the set other than the main entry.

Page numbers in parentheses—e.g., **1**: (24)—locate information in At-a-Glance boxes.

Animals that get main entries in the set are indexed under their common names, alternative common names, and scientific names.

Picture Credits

Abbreviations

FLPA — Frank Lane Picture Agency
OSF — Oxford Scientific Films

t = top; b = bottom; c = center; l = left; r = right

Jacket

tl caracal, Pete Oxford/naturepl.com; tr group of dolphins, Robert Harding Picture Library; bl lowland gorilla, Martin Rügner/Naturphotographie; br Rothchild's giraffe, Gerard Lacz/FLPA

9 Stephen J. Krasemann/Bruce Coleman Collection; **10–11** Peter Davey/FLPA; **12–13** K.G. Preston–Mafham/Premaphotos Wildlife; **15** Rafi Ben–Shahar/OSF; **18–19** Steve Turner/OSF; **21** Tom Vezo/naturepl.com; **22–23** Daniel J. Cox/OSF; **23** Bettmann/Corbis; **24, 24–25** Tom Ulrich/OSF; **26**t Ralph Reinhold/Animals Animals/OSF; **26**b Richard Day/OSF; **27** Wendy Shattil/Bob Rozinski/OSF; **28–29** Konrad Wothe/OSF; **30–31** Stan Osolinski/OSF; **33** Mark Hamblin/OSF; **35** Mark Deeble & Victoria Stone/OSF; **36–37** Jorge Sierra/OSF; **38** Press–Tige Pictures/OSF; **38–39** David Thompson/OSF; **40–41** Mark Hamblin/OSF; **41** Robin Redfern/OSF; **42** Tom Ulrich/OSF; **42–43** T. Leeson/Sunset/FLPA; **44–45** Mike Birkhead/OSF; **46–47** Alan & Sandy Carey/OSF; **48–49** Tom Ulrich/OSF; **50–51** Alan & Sandy Carey/OSF; **52–53** Marianne Wilding/Survival Anglia/OSF; **54** Dean Conger/Corbis; **55** Richard Packwood/OSF; **56–57, 57** Daniel J. Cox/OSF; **58–59** Niall Benvie/OSF; **60–61** Nick Gordon/OSF; **61** Niall Benvie/OSF; **62–63** Bridget Wheeler/Survival Anglia/OSF; **64–65** Joe McDonald/Animals Animals/OSF; **66** Alan & Sandy Carey/OSF; **66–67** Daniel J. Cox/OSF; **68–69** Nick Gordon/OSF; **70–71** Michael Leach/OSF; **72–73** Stan Osolinski/OSF; **73** Howard Hall/OSF; **74** Jeff Foott/Okapia/OSF; **75** Claude Steelman/Survival Anglia/OSF; **76–77** Bob Bennett/OSF; **78–79** Neil Latham/OSF; **79** David Fox/OSF; **80** Richard Packwood/OSF; **80–81** Robin Redfern/OSF; **82–83** Anthony Bannister/ABPL/OSF; **84–85** Richard Day/OSF; **86** TC Nature/OSF; **86–87** Zig Leszczynski/Animals Animals/OSF; **87** Daniel J. Cox/OSF; **89** Anup Shah/naturepl.com; **92–93** Gerard Lacz/FLPA; **94–95** Werner Pfunder/OSF; **96–97, 97** Doug Allan/OSF; **100–101, 102, 102–103, 103, 104–105** David Macdonald/OSF; **106–107** Adrian Bailey/OSF; **108–109** Belinda Wright/OSF; **110–111** Steve Turner/OSF

Artists

Denys Ovenden, Priscilla Barrett with Michael Long, Graham Allen, Malcolm McGregor

While every effort has been made to trace the copyright holders of illustrations reproduced in this book, the publishers will be pleased to rectify any omissions or inaccuracies.